How Jesus
Ended Up in the
Food Court

Seventy-Seven
Devotional Thoughts
You Never Thought About Before

By Doug Mendenhall

HUNTSVILLE TIMES

Published by

VMI PUBLISHERS

Partnering With Christian Authors, Publishing Christian and Inspirational Books

Sisters, Oregon
www.vmipublishers.com

ISBN: 1-933204-20-6

Library of Congress Control Number: 2006922969

Author Contact:
doug.mendenhall@htimes.com

DEDICATION

For my wife, Janet, and for Dr. Charlie Marler,
the two best editors in my world.

ABOUT THIS BOOK

The essays collected in this book originally appeared in *The Huntsville Times*, one of Alabama's daily newspapers, as my weekly "Soul Food" columns. They span the years 2000 to 2004; the original newspaper publication date precedes each piece. As far as is practical, the title for each essay is adapted from the original newspaper headline.

The latest "Soul Food" installment appears each week online at www.al.com/religion/huntsvilletimes/dmendenhall.ssf.

I am indebted to the editor of *The Times*, Melinda Gorham, for her consistent support and encouragement of my weekly endeavors; to the hundreds of readers who took time to tell me that "Soul Food" was an important part of their weekly diet; and to my sister, Jan Mendenhall, who helped this book come to life.

T A B L E   O F
C O N T E N T S

SECTION ONE:
I CAN ONLY IMAGINE

"For a thousand years in your sight are like a day that has just gone by, or like a watch in the night." Psalm 90:4

04.28.2001: Put a lifetime of thought into how you spend your momentary riches

A certain master had two servants. To each he gave a great treasure ... 38 million minutes.

"Use each minute as you will," the master told the two.

Now, 38 million minutes (633,333 hours) is far too much time for a man to measure. So one servant was at first extravagant. He grew addicted to hobbies that consumed much time. Leisure, he called it, and he leisurely poured buckets of time into it. His friends were envious but could not mimic his attitude. "After all," one told him, "time is money."

This is sound counsel, thought the servant, and he diverted his stream of time from playing to working. He invested heavily in a business career, and to his satisfaction found that indeed time could be leveraged into money.

Having discovered this, he ripped through his 38 million minutes (26,389 days) unwrapping each as fast as possible to get to the delicious wealth at its center.

Eventually this servant could not bear to sit idle, wasting time. He fumed about computer download times and hung up on answering machines if they took more than three seconds to beep.

On the way to the hospital with his third heart attack, his 38 million minutes (72 years) were used up, and he died.

But there was another servant. Because 38 million minutes is far too much time for a man to measure, at first this servant thought his time would last forever. "Well, if I am to be here forever, I had better find someone to share this time with me, or it will be a bleak and lonely 38 million minutes." So he found a mate, and loved her, and spent extravagant amounts of time with her, in golden moments and diamond days.

Eventually this servant saw that his treasure of time would not last forever, but upon reflection he realized he was happy with what each moment had purchased. He told his mate this, and she smiled knowingly. "After all," she said, "time is life."

The servant was blessed with friends and with children and with grandchildren, too. Though his treasure dwindled, he gave gifts from it still, and saw even strangers' eyes alight with the joy of his time.

His mate was with the servant when the light left his eyes. She knew his 38 million minutes (a lifetime) were used up, and mourned as he died.

Then the two servants were called before the master to account for how they'd spent their treasures.

To the first servant, who had sped past each minute in search of a brighter future, the master said, "Go now and be with others who view time as you do.

"You will be there forever."

"Forever?" the servant cried. "That will be hell!"

To the second servant, who had relished each minute given to others, the master said, "Come now and sit by me. We view time alike. You will stay here forever."

"Forever?" the servant exulted. "This will be heaven."

And so in 38 million minutes, two servants prepared for eternity.

"There is only one Lawgiver and Judge, the one who is able to save and destroy. But you – who are you to judge your neighbor?" James 4:12

07.14.2001: Making a list, checking it twice, then switching it would be nice

The Sunday school teacher gave out homework, a rarity. You actually completed it, a miracle.

The assignment wasn't hard: "Make a list of 10 people you'd like to see in heaven." A spouse. A child. Your parents. A favorite minister. You had 10 in a minute and a half, and they were already believers. Since the lesson had been on sharing the Good News, your homework was complete. These 10 had already been shared with. No sweat.

In fact, your show wouldn't be on TV for another couple minutes.

Possessed by some minor demon of tackiness, you turned the paper over and started another list: "Ten people I *wouldn't* like to see in heaven." That man-child who terrorized you in fifth grade. The vice president of sales. That too-serious T-ball coach who trampled your team into the red dust. That sour woman around the corner who stopped you for 15 minutes whenever you jogged past, complaining about her joints and bowels and warning you not to step on her grass.

Ten names popped onto the paper almost as quickly as the first list, and the theme music was just starting. You folded the paper, tucked it into the back of your Bible and forgot about it.

Seven days later, Sunday school began again. The teacher asked if anyone had finished the homework from last week. For once you could contribute, and it felt good to hand the list to him.

"Great," the teacher said. "It's good to see so many of you concerned about the lost. Let's just take time to read one list aloud, and we'll all join in prayer for those 10 souls."

He held up a creased sheet, and you knew it was yours. All right – a little perceived piety from your peers for an investment of 90 seconds was a good deal.

Then you remembered.

For a long moment you had the horrible feeling that comes before some car wrecks, when time slows down, but not enough for you to swerve and avoid the impact. On the side of the sheet away from the teacher you could read the names of your spouse, your kid, your parents. That meant ...

He began reading. Trapped, you slumped forward and closed your eyes. Your impressed classmates thought you must be praying, and from the distressed look on your face for the rest of the hour, they knew you took that list seriously.

Some wanted to help.

"That woman was my mom's best friend," said one. "I'll bet if we went to see her together, she'd be tickled to have the company. How's Tuesday?"

"He hasn't changed since fifth grade, but that guy lives on my block now," said another. "Some night next week come on over. We'll grill some burgers and invite his family, too."

You were trapped. What a nightmare. You nodded, gritted your teeth, forced a plastic smile and walked out of the building. As the offers kept coming, you looked toward the skies in exasperation.

And God smiled back. No plastic.

"For you know that it was not with perishable things such as silver or gold that you were redeemed from the empty way of life handed down to you from your forefathers, but with the precious blood of Christ." 1 Peter 1:18-19

01.26.2002: Even in fairy tales, there are things worth more than the Golden Touch

Not many people know this, but King Midas had a twin brother, Vitus, who, because he had no throne of his own, pursued other interests.

Midas was a fine character, but as you know he didn't become famous until he met a strange little man who claimed to have special powers. "I can give you the Golden Touch," Midas was told. "If you accept it, everything you touch will turn to gold."

Vitus was a fine character, too, but he met a different man who claimed to have special powers. "I can give you the Master's Touch," Vitas was told.

"If you accept it, every aspect of your life will be touched by him."

"Well, lay it on me," said Midas.

"Lay it on me," said Vitus.

Eager to test his new gift, Midas walked to a rose bush and reached out his finger to its red flower. Instantly it turned to gold and the branch that held it snapped under its new weight.

Eager to test his new gift, Vitas also walked to a garden. He had passed this way before, but now reached out his finger to the most beautiful red flower he had ever seen. Its color, its perfume and the silky touch of it snapped something in his heart. He knew that such beauty must have come from the Master.

Midas went inside and touched the bread and wine at his table. With the Golden Touch it became valuable, but tasteless.

Vitus went inside and touched the bread and wine at his table. With the Master's Touch it became a feast full of delicious meaning.

Still ecstatic, Midas ran to find his wife. The queen was a good woman – not, as you might expect, a gold digger – but when the happy king began to tell her of his new riches he touched her on the arm and felt her become cold.

Also ecstatic, Vitus ran to find his wife. She too was a good woman – although some people found her a bit cold – but when her happy husband began to tell her what the Master had done in his life, she felt a warmth spread from her heart. Soon she too had the Master's Touch, and it filled her with the same joy her husband knew.

You know the rest of the story of Midas, who ran about his kingdom touching everything he could get his hands on until his greed turned into irritation and then grief. When last we saw Midas he was searching desperately for that strange little man, to see if he could somehow undo the ruin spread by the Golden Touch.

The rest of the story of Vitus, though, is a bit different. To each aspect of his life he applied the Master's Touch – to his family, his friends, his daily work, his play, and, yes, even his gold. And as he spread that touch, the Master became more precious to him, a source of ever more joy.

Vitus never stopped using the Master's Touch, and was said to be happiest when he met some soul who had not yet experienced it. He touched many people in his life, and they all lived happily ever after.

Not counting Midas.

*"He who doubts is like a wave of the sea, blown and tossed by
the wind. That man should not think he will receive anything
from the Lord; he is a doubleminded man, unstable in
all he does." James 1:6-8*

10.04.2003: The fable of the flood and that nice guy in the middle

So there were these three guys. Maybe you knew them. Maybe you know somebody like them.

They all lived in the same neighborhood, went to the same schools, ate at the same restaurants, shopped at the same Wal-Mart, cut their grass on the same day of the week.

You might look at them and think they were cut from the same mold. You would be wrong.

For starters, Noah was sort of eccentric, especially when you first met him. That's because within the first 10 minutes, he would bring up the topic of the end of the world, and how he believed people were making a big mistake not turning to God and showing him how sorry they were for the many ways they'd messed up their lives.

He didn't scream about it, and I guess there's nothing inherently weird in talking about your religious beliefs, but Noah took it way past the point where it made for comfortable, low-stress conversation. I mean, he made it sound like it was a matter of life and death.

Melvin was pretty much the opposite in that regard. He mentioned God maybe more often than Noah, but always with a big exclamation point and a couple of red-hot curses after the name.

He probably hung around Noah just to razz him, to make sure Noah knew how little stock Melvin put in all that end-of-the-world talk.

Actually, I don't know why Noah let him hang around at all, because Melvin was pretty much a lowlife. Eighty percent of the neighborhood believed with 80 percent confidence that the guy beat his wife. He was a slobbering mess at parties. If you loaned him a tool you might find it a week later in a pawn shop.

The third guy was Phil. The best way to describe Phil is to say he was sort of a cross between Noah and Melvin. Or you might say that Phil was the glue that held these three guys together.

Phil could nod his head and look like he was thinking deep thoughts when Noah went off on one of his tirades about how people had better start repenting of their wicked ways. Then a minute later he could slap Melvin on the back, laugh at one of his gross stories and say, "Melvin, you old dog, you."

Phil tried to make everyone comfortable. Well, actually, I don't think Phil tried – he just naturally fit in with whoever was around.

I'm sure you know most of the story of what finally happened to these three guys. How it turned out Noah was right and there really was a flood to wipe evil from the face of the Earth. How Melvin was one of the first to drown, being hung over and in a state of denial even when the water was up to his neck.

No surprise there.

But what happened to Phil, that guy in the middle, the only one in this fable that you and I can identify with?

Well, when he got to the door of the ark, it turned out they already had two chameleons aboard.

The door closed, and Phil had a sudden sinking feeling.

"Some people are like seed along the path, where the word is sown. As soon as they hear it, Satan comes and takes away the word that was sown in them." Mark 4:15

07.19.2003: The devil's new hymnal didn't get rid of the classics

Maybe you haven't heard, but the devil finally finished revising "Hell's Hymnal." A lot of churches go through this long and painful process, culling out the moldy songs nobody sings anyway and making room for the catchy new ones.

In the devil's case, this process took even longer than usual, because the changes had to be approved by a subcommittee, a full committee, a review committee and a leadership committee. The devil just loves committees.

Anyway, the new hymnal is finally on its way to the printer, and as usual nobody is happy with the results. Either their favorite song was cut or some new one they can't stand was added. Hell's minions will be bickering about this for years.

Don't worry, though. Some of the true classics survived and will continue to be sung often – if off-key – wherever the devil's work is done.

To name a few:

"All Things Bright and Beautiful (the Lord God made the mall)."

"On Jordan's Stormy Banks I Stand (and worry about getting my shoes wet)."

"Jesus Loves the Little Children (but adults are too busy for that sort of thing)."

"Amazing Grace (how illogical the concept)."

"God of Our Fathers (is hopelessly out of touch with today's problems)."

"Sex Lifted Me (so who needs love?)."

"Just a Little Talk With Jesus (once a year is plenty for me)."

"How Great Thou Art (thou remarkable human being, thou)."

"Beautiful Isle of Somewhere (A cruise would cure all my problems)."

"For Unto Us a Child Is Born (and as responsible parents we will no longer have time for church events)."

"Clap Your Hands, All Ye People (football season's finally here)."

"Come Ye Disconsolate (and dwell on how hard you have it)."

"I Am a Poor Wayfaring Stranger (and nobody around here understands how hard I have it)."

"Does Jesus Care? (Not really)."

"Eternal Father, Strong to Save (but not till I'm closer to the grave)."

"Unto the Hills Around Do I Lift Up My Longing Eyes (and wish I owned that house up there)."

"A Shelter in the Time of Storm (but that's the only time)."

"Give Me the Bible (I need a book that will look good on the coffee table next to Southern Living)."

"Watch and Pray (that TV doesn't have any lasting effects on your mind)."

"How Shall the Young Secure Their Hearts (unless I give them everything their hearts desire?)."

"In Christ There Is No East or West (but I'll bet he loves my country best)."

"Lo! What a Glorious Sight Appears (and there's nothing wrong with a guy watching the ladies)."

"Just As I Am (is going to have to be good enough 'cause I'm sure not changing)."

Now, it's true that not many Christian mouths have sung these hymns the way they appear in the devil's hymnal, but don't tell me that Christian minds haven't thought them that way.

Why, the devil even set up a committee that studied the matter and concluded that this kind of mouth-to-mind discord is way more effective than backward masking.

*"How beautiful on the mountains are the feet of those who
bring good news, who proclaim peace, who bring good tidings,
who proclaim salvation, who say to Zion, 'Your God reigns!'"*

Isaiah 52:7

12.16.2000: For years Mary could close her eyes and still see his beautiful feet

He was her first baby, and she was mesmerized by his every sigh, every cry, every shudder and start.

Even when he was asleep she had a hard time leaving him alone. She loved the way his toe flexed upward if she stroked the tiny sole of his foot. She even loved the way he convulsed at a sudden noise – although the first time it frightened her so that she gasped and clutched him to her breast.

She was tired, and sometimes she wasn't sure whether she was awake and watching her baby, or nodding off and dreaming of him. Either way, she was at peace ...

Mary opened her eyes with a start, confused for a second by a scene she could no longer avoid. The screams, the laughter, the blood and the pain.

The legionnaire was finished hammering now, and the spike held Jesus' feet to the wood despite his convulsions. Mary's mind had fled before the image of the hammer swinging toward Jesus, back to a time when those feet were unmarked. She could kiss and tickle those feet and look into eyes that still did not know pain. She wanted to be back there again, not here.

As they raised the cross, Mary couldn't look full at her son. Her gaze stopped no higher than his tortured feet.

Mary had watched those feet grow, usually bare but sometimes in sandals that were too soon outgrown. She had seen those feet skip and jump in play. She had seen them with heels raised and toes curled in the dust, as Jesus knelt to help Joseph with some project. Or as he knelt to pray. She had seen that many times.

In the last several years she had seen other people fall and grab Jesus by the feet, pleading for a bit of his power.

Jairus, the synagogue ruler, who wanted his little girl rescued from death. That horrible man Legion, full of demons when he met Jesus, although now it wouldn't surprise her to turn and see Legion softly crying at the crucifixion of his exorcist. A Samaritan leper, to whom Jesus gave skin like that of a newborn.

There was another Mary, Lazarus' sister, who rubbed Jesus' dusty feet with more perfume than his mother had seen since accepting the magi's gifts as she cradled him.

Jesus groaned, and at last Mary looked up. Then she could not look away. Their eyes met, and Jesus rasped out: "John, take care of my mother. Love her like a son."

John did. The gentle man led her away from the cross and got her through the darkest hours. He comforted her until the empty tomb made life livable again.

Years passed. Mary still shuddered at times when she'd see again a moment from that day at the cross, like the instant of the hammer arcing toward Jesus' feet.

But Mary smiled, too. Sometimes the smile meant she was back in Bethlehem. Sometimes the smile came when Scripture was read as she sat with other believers.

One verse that brought the smile was from Isaiah: "How beautiful are the feet of those who bring good news."

Mary liked that a lot.

"Let us fix our eyes on Jesus, the author and perfecter of our faith, who for the joy set before him endured the cross, scorning its shame, and sat down at the right hand of the throne of God."

Hebrews 12:2

03.30.2002: Heavenly thoughts while waiting for that stone to roll into place

They looked down through the clouds, or around the curve of space, or across the millions of miles, or however it is that heaven and Earth are bridged. They looked and they saw Jesus, carried lifeless from the cross to the grave.

Even in heaven there was no escaping the horror of the moment.

Jonah remembered the slimy darkness and the sour smell of the fish's belly. He knew that three days could seem an eternity.

David thought for a moment of his beautiful son, Absalom, hanging dead from a tree. Then his quick mind flitted among a dozen lyrics he'd written, settling on "The enemy pursues me, he crushes me to the ground; he makes me dwell in darkness like those long dead."

Caleb remembered the decades spent watching every one of his peers die around him in the desert, until only he and Joshua were left. They were imperfect too, he knew, but God spared them. Yet now this perfect son of God, who shared Joshua's name, was not to be spared.

Noah heard again the shouts and screams from outside the barred door of the ark. The storm eventually drowned out those awful noises. But now it was Jesus who was outside, and the door had been slammed shut once again.

Eve saw again the faces of her two oldest sons, the hatred on Cain's and the blankness on Abel's as he lay there silently in a pool of blood. She and Adam had been the first parents to see a son die, and now here it was happening again with God's son. His only son.

Moses realized anew the gift God had given him at life's end, showing him the rich promised land, staying by him until his eyes closed, then gently burying him in a private spot. How unlike Moses' own death was the rough treatment Jesus had received.

Samson wished mightily that he had the strength to stop what was happening, but knew that muscles were not the answer.

Methuselah calculated quietly. Jesus was so young that it would take 30 of his lifetimes to equal Methuselah's record span of 969 years. So quickly it was over for Jesus – but with so much achieved. If I'd lived 30 times as long as I did, thought Methuselah, I'd not have accomplished as much.

Elijah, brought to heaven by a whirlwind in a chariot of fire, noticed that there was not even a breeze whispering in the heavy darkness that surrounded Jesus.

John, the newcomer, cried at the sight of his cousin. I tried to tell them, he thought, but could I have tried harder?

And what of Abraham, the one they all called "Father of the Faithful?"

Abraham was remembering the promise, the one God had made to him in Haran when so much of the journey was ahead of him: "All peoples on earth will be blessed through you." What an amazing promise, he thought, not for the first time. And at what a terrible price."

From far below came the crash of a huge stone rolling into place. Together, they looked down and waited.

"They waited for me as for showers and drank in my words as the spring rain. When I smiled at them, they scarcely believed it; the light of my face was precious to them." Job 29:23-24

03.06.2004: Angels agree that beautiful days belong in the spring

God is smart enough not to rely much on committees. He's used them now and then, of course, such as the committee that designed the platypus. That's one group of angels that never really meshed.

Then there's the Perennial Task Force on the Four Seasons, which meets to iron out details of the calendar and the weather. The heavy lifting of this group was finished thousands of years ago, and most folks think it did a pretty good job of fulfilling God's original directive to put some variety into the year. "Turn, turn, turn," he told the leaders of the four subcommittees, "Keep it moving. These people get bored quickly."

However, God never told the task force to stop meeting, so it still convenes every year.

If you've ever served on a committee or jury with somebody who is in no hurry to wrap things up, imagine how the meetings drag on when every member is immortal and has no real concept of time.

For about a century now they've been wrangling over whether to switch to the term "autumn" instead of "fall." The chairman of the Fall Subcommittee points out that, "When people – or angels – hear 'The Fall,' they think of, well, you know." Nobody really disagrees with him, but he still hasn't been able to convince a majority to go along with the change.

Another hot topic of discussion is how hot to make the summer. One faction thinks it should be merely warm, while the other thinks if you cranked up the thermostat 20 degrees, more people would break into a sweat about trying to avoid a permanent hell.

But the longest debate is how to fairly divvy up each year's allotment of holidays and beautiful weather. The Winter Subcommittee, for example, has agreed to get by with just two or three beautiful days in exchange for keeping control of Christmas, which is considered a real plum.

The autumn angels annually try to pry extra days away from summer, which fires up the Summer Subcommittee. It's an even battle, so some years one group wins and some years the other. "Indian summer" is a temporary compromise still being studied.

The lion's share of the most perfect days of the year, though, always end up in the hands of the Spring Subcommittee. A while back, a newcomer to the Winter Subcommittee tried to make a name for himself by speaking out against this inequity.

"Why should spring get all of the best weather?" he asked. "I mean, it's not like they don't have their share of holidays, too. Spring has May Day, Arbor Day, St. Patrick's Day, spring break, Easter ..."

Then the rookie's voice trailed off. The rest of the committee just stared at him quietly until he realized he'd answered his own question.

The committee moves Easter around each year, but as long as it is sometime in the spring, not an angel in heaven will object to the most beautiful, perfect days being clustered around this holiday of perfect joy and perfect sorrow.

Every year, the vote's unanimous to let Easter shine.

"Now the LORD God had planted a garden in the east, in Eden; and there he put the man he had formed. And the LORD God made all kinds of trees grow out of the ground — trees that were pleasing to the eye and good for food." Genesis 2:8-94

07.05.2003: Where can the Lord go for a vacation so perfect?

The good Lord was thinking about taking a vacation, maybe just a four-day weekend to get away from it all.

Several of the angels suggested a tour of the gardens of Palestine. "It's beautiful country – flowing with milk and honey," said Gabriel.

"You don't get out much, do you?" the Lord said. "Flowing with blood and guts these days."

Somebody else described a bed and breakfast they'd heard about up in Pennsylvania Dutch country, with great apple pancakes and a choice of two hammocks on the back porch and a third down by a little creek. "I don't know," the Lord said. "Can you see me in a hammock?"

The angels tried to be helpful, really they did. I mean, they worship the big guy and they wanted him to be happy.

So how about fly fishing in Montana? "Well … I hear the steelhead are pretty fair sized, but ask Jonah to show you the pictures from our deep-sea trip – now that was a big fish!"

Maybe you could take in a few Broadway plays in the Big Apple. "There hasn't been one with a decent plot since 'Fiddler on the Roof.' Besides, I'm pretty sure that 'Big Apple' nickname has something to do with the serpent, doesn't it? I have to be careful what I endorse."

Good point, sir. But how about an eco-friendly expedition to Costa Rica? Birds, flowers, exotic wildlife? "Sounds lovely, but it's pretty depressing when you realize there's only a few acres of garden left out of all I made."

Maybe a nice cruise? They say there's nothing as wide as a Caribbean sunset. "Except the buffet table. Gluttony isn't supposed to be at the top of my to-do list, you know."

You could try Disney World. "I'll pass. Every time I hear someone calling my name and turn around it turns out they're just commenting on the length of the lines."

How about touring Washington, D.C.? There's the Smithsonian, the monuments, the Capitol. "Oh, right, that's all I need is for someone in Washington to think it's my favorite vacation spot. Those Americans already have enough of a superiority complex as it is."

The mountains? "Too close to home."

The beach? "Too many condos."

A golf resort? "That game would make even me lose faith in me."

"I don't mean to be out of line, sir," said Gabriel, "but maybe you're being a little too picky? I mean, after all, no place is perfect, is it?"

"Once upon a time, Gabriel, once upon a time," the good Lord said. "You remember Eden, don't you? The animals, the flowers, the rivers? And those long walks every evening with my people. That was the last decent vacation I had."

"I remember, sir," Gabriel said, a catch in his voice. "It was the last decent vacation your people had, too."

"True enough," the Lord said. "And you know, Gabriel, I'd do just about anything to get things back to the way they were. Just about anything."

SECTION TWO:
THE OLD TESTAMENT

"What is man that you make so much of him, that you give him
so much attention, that you examine him every morning
and test him every moment?" Job 7:17-18

08.09.2003: What fills all of the years before and
after this Earth?

It seems irrelevant to talk about how old Earth is – Earth and
the rest of the universe. Whether you measure that age in
thousands, millions or billions of years, the important question is
whether the universe is finite.

That is, whether God, who is infinite, started the thing up.

Because if he did, and if he also plans to end the thing some
day, that means Earth and the universe around it are merely one
segment in the endless chain of time.

You know how cinematographers like to show you a close-
up of a character, then pan back and back and back until the
character becomes a speck in a vast landscape, then finally
disappears as the camera goes back even more?

You can do the same thing in thinking about the age of the
universe. If the universe is a billion years old you can think about
infinity as a trillion years and the universe seems but a moment.
If the universe is a trillion years...well, you can play this game
forever, panning back and back.

Or at least God can play it forever. You are even more finite
than the Earth, and your mind quickly cramps from trying to
understand infinity and turns instead to fashion or football or
what's for lunch.

But before that happens, think about infinity for just a
moment longer. Because what I want to know is, if the time span
of Earth is like a single paper clip in a chain of paper clips that
stretches from the far side of the sun to the far side of the moon
and beyond, what happens in all the rest of that time before and
after?

If trillions of centuries stretch out before the creation of this
universe and quintillions more are planned after it is snuffed out,

with what activities does God the creator fill that time? I can ask this question because I am a self-centered mortal, and as such cannot possibly understand what there would be to do outside of my physical universe.

Surely those heptillions of years aren't just filled with hallelujahs and halos and everyone crowded around God's throne? I can ask this question because I don't know enough about God to understand how simply being in his presence could be the most complete existence I could ask for. And I can ask this question because I have such a short attention span that I want there to be more action, more plot.

I realize that my shortcomings are what drive my questions. It is not that God makes no sense, but that I don't have the sense to fathom him.

Still, the thought of a timeline that runs flat for trillions of years before the blip of Earth's existence and then runs flat again for sextillions of years more after it is gone makes me wonder. Has God the Creator done all of this before, with other universes? Or will he do it all again someday, when I have become an angel able to look over his shoulder and admire his handiwork more appropriately?

It's awfully hard to think about such things, stuck as I am in this body that gets dizzy just watching a movie in which the camera zooms back and back and back. But I think he likes it when I try.

"When Pharaoh saw that there was relief, he hardened his heart and would not listen to Moses and Aaron, just as the LORD had said." Exodus 8:15

06.01.2002: Maybe this is my favorite plague because I know the feeling so well

Just because I have a favorite plague, that doesn't make me a masochist, does it?

My favorite color is blue, my favorite dessert is lemon meringue pie, my favorite Bible verse is Isaiah 12:3, and my favorite joke is "How many boring people does it take to change a light bulb? One."

But I also have a favorite among the 10 plagues with which God smacked down Pharaoh, back when Moses was his foreman.

It's not the plague of boils; that's too disgusting.

It's not the death of the firstborn; that's too grim.

(Incidentally, back during Passover, I got a cheerful flier from the Jewish Community Center of Milwaukee, titled "Ways to Liven Up the Seder." It suggests making "plague bags" for the kids containing little trinkets to jog their memories about the holiday – Styrofoam balls for the hail, sunglasses for the darkness, etc. The list ends with "Death of the firstborn: You may consider skipping this." Good advice.)

No, my favorite plague is frogs.

For starters, I like the inherent comedy of the scene. As Moses promised Pharaoh, the frogs came "into your palace and your bedroom and onto your bed, into the houses of your officials and on your people, and into your ovens and kneading troughs." The 7-year-old boy in me wants to see that, to hear the shrieks of Mrs. Pharaoh and her prissy princesses.

During my last trip to Florida, a lizard crawled inside my pillowcase one night and I discovered it early in the morning, fidgeting under my ear. This made for a very effective alarm clock. Let's just say the plague of frogs was a concentrated form of the lizard-in-the-bed incident.

A more ironic humor is added to the story by Pharaoh's magicians. Faced with an escalating frog crisis, they take pride in the fact they can make frogs appear, too. Why do I think this wasn't exactly what Pharaoh had in mind when he turned to these bureaucrats for help?

In the end, Pharaoh realizes that only the Lord can help him. He appeals to Moses, who tells him, "I leave to you the honor of setting the time for me to pray for you and your officials and your people that you and your houses may be rid of the frogs."

Say the word and there'll be relief from these slimy little things making you so miserable. The obvious answer is, "Just do it!"

That's what you'd say, right? If you knew happiness could come only when you asked God for relief from some sin, habit, pressure or problem hopping through your life, you wouldn't say what Pharaoh said, would you?

You can look up his one-word answer in Exodus 8:10.

"Tomorrow," Pharaoh said.

Maybe he just had a frog in his throat.

But there's nothing funny about deciding to put up with the frogs for another day when you could be rid of them immediately.

One word for a person who lives like that is procrastinator.

Another word is masochist.

*"And the LORD said to Samuel: 'See, I am about to do
something in Israel that will make the ears of everyone who
hears of it tingle.'" 1 Samuel 3:11*

08.14.2004: Baby Samuel found a gift
worth more than he lost

It is a sad story, or at least a bittersweet one. It stars a good,
graceful woman, doted on by her husband. Hannah was a good
woman, but indescribably sad because she wanted more than
anything to be a mother.

Her husband's other woman, the fertile Peninnah, made
matters worse, taunting Hannah to tears about her lack of babies.

One day Hannah stood outside the temple, distraught and
disheveled from a long cry, her lips moving silently as she prayed
that God would send her a son. She looked like a wasted drunk,
so the priest told her to move along and sober up. Hannah
explained herself: "I have not been drinking wine or beer; I was
pouring out my soul to the Lord."

That touched old Eli, the priest, so he told her God would
grant whatever she'd been praying for.

Nine months later she was holding the thing she'd wanted
more than anything in this world, her baby boy, Samuel. If she
was drunk now, it was with joy. Her song praising the Lord fills
most of the second chapter of 1 Samuel.

Only one problem. In her despair Hannah had vowed that if
God would give her a son "I will give him to the Lord for all the
days of his life." So as soon as baby Samuel was weaned, Hannah
delivered him to Eli, to live in the temple for the rest of his life.

It makes a tidy Sunday school story. In fact, it was the
Sunday school story last week, when I was assisting my wife
with her first-grade class. The children liked it.

They seemed unbothered by the question that enters my mind
every time I hear the tale of Hannah and Samuel: How could a
mother – who ached for a son so badly – let him go so soon, to
be raised by a stranger and visited by his mommy only once a

year? How could her husband, Elkanah, allow her to go through with the vow? How could a loving God expect such a sacrifice? How could Eli?

I am not the first parent who has read this Bible story and asked those questions.

There is an answer, thankfully, and it is a good one.

In the middle of one night in his lonely bed in the temple, the very voice that spoke the universe into existence now spoke the name of Samuel. And as soon as he had the boy's attention, he told him, "I am about to do something in Israel that will make the ears of everyone who hears of it tingle."

This was the first of many conversations Samuel had with the Lord Almighty, conversations about important, world-changing events. I expect Samuel's ears still tingle when God speaks to him.

And with that first conversation between the future prophet and the eternal God, my questions about how Hannah could have given up Samuel are answered in full.

Even first-graders can understand if you explain it simply. The answer comes in the form of another question, one worth asking every day:

Is there anything in this world you would not give up, for the chance to hear God speak your name?

"Posterity will serve him; future generations will be told about the Lord. They will proclaim his righteousness to a people yet unborn – for he has done it." Psalm 22:30-31

03.23.2002: Only one man is left who knows the tune to 'The Deer of the Dawn'

Maybe it's a good thing that we've lost the tune to that mournful old song, "The Deer of the Dawn." Just reading the lyrics is hard enough to take.

Some people think Jesus was singing that song in the Garden of Gethsemane while he waited for the gang of bloodthirsty thugs he knew was on its way, led by his friend Judas.

You can't really tell by the sketchy narration of the Gospels whether Jesus was singing the whole song or reciting it or whether he just cried out the first few words to remind God of all that the following verses said would happen.

Two souls who know each other really well can carry on shorthand conversations that way, like old married people who seem to share telepathy.

But the first line is all that's recorded in Matthew and Mark. You've probably heard it before: "My God, my God, why have you forsaken me?"

If you want to read the whole thing, it is included in the Bible as Psalm 22. King David wrote this song, borrowing the tune to "The Deer of the Dawn," and even without the instrumentation or the melody it can be a gripping piece of poetry.

But reading it and thinking about Jesus huddled alone in the middle of the night and singing it to his father will send a chill up your spine.

"Do not be far from me, for trouble is near and there is no one to help."

Sometimes people worry about Jesus' emotional state during this unguarded moment in the garden. It doesn't seem right for the one who is supposed to be perfect to cry out in pain about God turning his back. Has Jesus lost his faith, or his nerve? Is he trying to welch on the deal that brought him to Earth in the first place? Would he really avoid the cross if God allowed it?

And what about his question, God? Why are you deserting him, leaving your son alone when he needs you so desperately? What kind of God are you, anyway?

It's an intense moment, sure, but those troubling questions disappear when you follow the song to its conclusion.

Yes, in the early verses the situation is dismal and hopeless: "O my God, I cry out by day, but you do not answer, by night, and am not silent."

As with all stories, you can't have a happy ending without a gloomy middle. Midway into the psalm, the tone changes: "He has not despised or disdained the suffering of the afflicted one; he has not hidden his face from him but has listened to his cry for help."

And because of what Jesus went through in the garden and on the cross, as scholar F.F. Bruce points out, if you or I feel God-forsaken and cry out, now there's somebody up there specifically to hear our mournful songs.

The last line of Psalm 22 says, "Future generations will be told about the Lord. They will proclaim his righteousness to a people yet unborn – for he has done it."

That means this song is written to us, doesn't it?

It makes a nice Easter gift.

"Joshua said to them, 'Do not be afraid; do not be discouraged. Be strong and courageous'." Joshua 10:25

05.21.2001: Let's go stand in front of a chariot and talk about trusting God

The chariot was obsolete long ago, before three millennia of military progress created so many jobs in high-tech Huntsville.

But in its day, the iron chariot was scary. Its hubcaps were sharpened like scythes, its horses were trained to trample, and its elite driver was meaner than a NASCAR veteran with a vendetta.

The new nation of Israel found independence only after Egypt's chariots lost their wheels in the Red Sea. And 40 years later, God led Israel to a land filled with more chariots.

After Israel's military victories against walled cities such as Jericho, the surviving kings of Palestine decided to roll out the chariots and squash these invaders. This shaped up as a worse mismatch than Gen. Schwarzkopf's forces against the halfhearted Iraqis.

But God told Joshua, "Do not be afraid of them, because by this time tomorrow I will hand all of them over to Israel, slain."

Jehovah had delivered these people before, and he came through again. But there still was an icy moment when the infantry of Israel had to stand out there on the plains while the chariots came racing straight at them.

That moment was critical to Israel's success, because it was in that moment that each man knew victory could not possibly come from his own arsenal.

That moment was inspirational, so David sang about it in one of the Psalms: "Some trust in chariots and some in horses, but we trust in the name of the Lord our God."

We still sing about that kind of trust, claiming we have it, but we also do our best to avoid that naked moment of standing there while the ground shakes from incoming chariots.

The victorious Israelites were told to destroy their enemies' horses and chariots to show their contempt for them, to show that with God on their side they had no need for an armored corps.

And if you were in the Jewish camp, you couldn't ride around in a chariot and yet argue you were still a wholehearted follower of God. Even if you said, "Well, it depends on what you use it for."

Later, the great kings of Israel had plenty of chariots of their own. But as Israel's visible armor grew mightier, the invisible armor supplied by God weakened. In the long run the people were better off with God than with the chariots.

Which brings me, finally, to a point.

The song I sing occasionally in church about trusting in God and not in chariots has a second verse that says, "some trust in the wealth of things," and a third that says, "some trust in the work they do."

But if I couldn't sing the first verse back then while standing in my own chariot, how can I sing the second and third verses today while hiding behind the shield of a 401(k), a good retirement plan and all of the other defensive weapons that most Christians call "good stewardship"?

I worry about this from time to time, and it always leaves me feeling like I've been run over by … something.

"And we know that in all things God works for the good of those who love him." Romans 8:28

07.07.2001: If you believe in God, you can't ask him not to get your hopes up

No kindness will go unpunished.

Maybe that saying was born on the lips of a woman who lived in the town of Shunem, back in biblical days.

She was a nice lady, with a nice husband, a nice house and a guest room that she spiffed up nicely so that a traveling preacher named Elisha could spend the night when he passed through.

Wanting to repay this kindness, Elisha asked what he could do for her. Put in a good word with the king? She demurred, so he asked for suggestions from his sidekick, Gehazi. "Well," Gehazi said, "she has no son and her husband is old."

That settled it. Elisha informed the kind woman that within a year she'd have a son.

"No, my lord," she objected. Maybe she was still just being polite, maybe she really didn't want a baby. Anyway, a year later she was a mother. Back then this was a cause for celebration – today it would more likely lead to suits against Elisha and Gehazi in both civil and criminal courts.

So the couple in Shunem now had an heir, and another Old Testament story could be wrapped up with a happy ending. Except that one day a few years later the boy went out to help his dad in the fields and complained of a headache. A field hand brought him to his mother, and she held him on her lap until he died.

Can there be a blacker sadness than hers in those few hours? Maybe she spent them humming lullabies. Maybe she rocked him. Maybe her tears wet his hair.

But soon he was gone, this little boy she never expected but now couldn't live without. She put his body on the bed in the guest room and went looking for Elisha.

She found him and spoke from a broken heart. "Did I ask you for a son, my lord?" she said. "Didn't I tell you, 'Don't raise my hopes?'"

Into your own life, God is going to send gifts. For starters, he's going to make things work out well for you although it will be on his schedule, not yours.

Some of his gifts will be with you for a lifetime; others will be gone before you're through with them. Those will be the ones you mourn, since you won't be able to take them for granted any longer.

Now, there's not much comfort you can give a parent who loses a child, whether in biblical days or the 21st century, so we shouldn't hold the poor woman responsible for words she spoke in her grief.

But maybe we can learn a little bit from her. If God holds out a gift or an opportunity, and if you refuse to take it or act on it because you're afraid of what might happen, it's a lot like saying to him, "Don't raise my hopes."

And that's a bad attitude to have toward life or toward God. Do you really think you'd be better off without his gifts, living a blander but safer existence?

Incidentally, Elisha went into the guest room and brought the dead boy back to life. This story does have a happy ending, with a mother who was glad she'd let God get her hopes up.

*"For you who revere my name, the sun of righteousness will
rise with healing in its wings. And you will go out and leap like
calves released from the stall." Malachi 4:2*

06.12.2004: If you find the church doors
locked, read Malachi

Dozens of other hints and second-hand paraphrasings say
virtually the same thing, so it's not like anybody in Palestine
could pretend they hadn't already gotten the message.

Still, only one time in the span of the Old Testament does
Jehovah God come straight out and say to his people, in exactly
these words, "I am not pleased with you."

That is a chilling sentence when you consider that it is uttered
by someone who, in the words of Bill Cosby, "brought you into
this world and can take you out of it." It is simple,
straightforward and direct. It is a sentence you expect to hear a
parent speak to a 4-year-old who has been coloring so far outside
the lines that the living room wall has become a Crayola mural.

And the good Lord, in his great patience, waits until the final
book of the Old Testament to mouth that sentence.

Maybe we should study the setting in that little book of
Malachi, where God says, "I am not pleased with you," and do
what we can to steer clear of the same mistakes. To be scared
straight is the beginning of wisdom, as King Solomon once
wrote, sort of.

Malachi was writing a century after Jerusalem had been
repopulated by settlers from Babylon, who'd been freed and sent
home after 70 years of slavery. Their parents and grandparents
had rebuilt the temple, rebuilt the walls of the war-flattened city,
rebuilt their own homes, rebuilt the ancient system of worship.

Those wild, frontier days were gone, though, and now the
people were bored with their comfortable lives and their
predictable, half-hearted worship. They went through the
motions, because it was the socially acceptable thing to do, but
they did so with sighs and yawns. If wristwatches had been

invented, they'd have looked at them all during the weekly service, judging the minutes left until lunch.

The priests were just like the laymen in this jaded, "sniffing" attitude. They said it was OK to replace wives with younger, more glamorous pagan models. They said it was OK to replace a prime head of livestock with a half-dead sheep and sacrifice it to God. They said it was OK to replace heartfelt tithing with occasional little offerings. They said it was OK to act like this because God wasn't going to do anything about it anyway.

God had a different view, so in Malachi he said, "Oh, that one of you would shut the temple doors, so that you would not light useless fires on my altar! I am not pleased with you, and I will accept no offering from your hands."

It's doesn't take a leap of logic to conclude that if God says again, "I am not pleased with you," it might be to another bunch who are bored with worship, who compartmentalize their spirituality so it doesn't spill into their business and personal lives and who want to worship greed and God at the same time.

I'm not speculating as to who that bunch might be, but if I get to church some Sunday morning and the doors are locked, I for one am going to be very afraid.

SECTION THREE:
THE NEW TESTAMENT

"While he was still a long way off, his father saw him and was filled with compassion for him; he ran to his son, threw his arms around him and kissed him." Luke 15:20

07.29.2000: True message about prodigal's welcomed return often gets missed

Just for the record, the prodigal son did not come home because he saw the error of his riotous ways and resolved to straighten up and fly right.

He ran out of money.

If not for empty pockets, which on the bright side gave him a fantastic weight-loss program, the prodigal son might have kept living large for a lifetime.

This is a point overlooked or downplayed in most sermons – that drinking and partying and throwing money at the exotic women of a far country is an awful lot of fun. And in the prodigal's case as in our own, it's not as if chasing your every whim suddenly becomes tiresome.

It's addictive.

In the movie "The War of the Roses," Mommy Rose indulges her two children in as much candy as they want, on the theory that it will get the craving out of their systems. Instead they grow into a couple of fat adults with sticky lips.

Now, it's true that most people imitating the prodigal's proclivities run out of money. Or energy.

Or they attend a few funerals, like surviving alumni of "Saturday Night Live," and decide it's time to rein in their recklessness. The epiphany of mortality has put a damper on a lot of carefree existences. Of course, it's also made a lot of people party harder, determined to create enough momentum to defeat gravity and float on mythic clouds of happiness.

But eventually, even if he'd invested part of his inheritance in mutual funds to avoid that embarrassing cash-flow crisis, the prodigal son would have looked around the joint one night and bemoaned, "All my rowdy friends have settled down."

That's not the point, though.

Jesus didn't make up the story about the prodigal son to convince the crowd that they'd better behave themselves or bad things would happen. He didn't tell it to affirm lessons from the fable of the ant and the grasshopper, or the tortoise and the hare.

He told it because he wanted his audience to know that they have a father figure in God himself, and that as a father, God is longing for the day when his lost boys and girls will come home. He has left a light in the window for them, but wants to do more. He has spent days standing at the front door, but wants to do more. So he has walked often down the long driveway to the mailbox, checking for a postcard or for the first glimpse of his children's return.

He wants to do more, but he knows it won't work to chase down the prodigals while they're still whooping it up in the far country. He can't drag them back. So he just keeps watching, ready the instant they decide they want to come home. That's what the lesson of the prodigal son is all about. No matter where you go, you can come home again. Even if you smell like pig slop, God the father will invite you into his house with an arm across your shoulders.

Now, as you walk in, some religious brothers and sisters sitting on the couch may hold their noses, but you'll just have to let God deal with them.

Don't worry; there was a time they didn't smell so great, either.

"Then the angel showed me the river of the water of life, as clear as crystal, flowing from the throne of God and of the Lamb down the middle of the great street of the city. On each side of the river stood the tree of life, bearing twelve crops of fruit, yielding its fruit every month. And the leaves of the tree are for the healing of the nations." Revelation 22:1-2

09:16.2000: From Genesis to Revelation and beyond, a river runs through it

As you wait for the summer drought to break, think about the spiritual importance of water.

The first image in the Bible is of the Spirit of God hovering over dark, unformed waters, preparing to create our world. The last image in the Bible – before John signs off with a note from the author – is of the river that flows through downtown Heaven.

And as you flip pages in this book bounded by Genesis and Revelation, you'll see that a river runs through it:

To begin the trip to their promised land, the ancient Israelites have to cross the miraculously parted waters of the Red Sea. They don't balk, what with the rear-view incentive of oncoming chariots.

But to seal the end of the trip, they have to repeat that crossing at the Jordan River.

With no bloodthirsty despots to spur them forward, there's time to look before leaping. Which they probably do, because at this spot the Jordan doesn't allow wading gradually into gentle shallows. The water's deep, the bank is steep, and Moses isn't around to hold out his staff and get the miracle started.

So picture yourself as a Jewish priest on the shore, hoisting the gold-laden Ark of the Covenant, wearing clothing too heavy for treading water.

You know the river will be at least up to your neck, but Jehovah has said that if you step in, it will dry up. That first step is going to be a doozy. Most steps of faith are.

To begin his string of public miracles, Jesus saves the day at a wedding reception in Cana by turning six huge jars of water into fine wine.

To begin his public ministry, Jesus is baptized in the Jordan. Think of that glorious instant when you break the surface after diving into a pool on a sunny day. For Jesus, that instant is one of the rare times God, so proud of his son, actually speaks from the clouds.

To begin spreading his ministry beyond the Jews, Jesus asks a woman from Samaria for a drink of water. He promises to give her the "water of life."

She doesn't have a clue what he means, but is so impressed that she leaves him at the well and runs off to tell all her friends.

To end the spread of evil on the earth, God covers it with water. Of course, as soon as he gets off that ark and has time to grow some grapes, Noah gets drunk. Guess he should have stuck to water.

To end Roman responsibility for what's about to happen to an innocent man, Pilate washes his hands.

To end the life of Jesus, a spear jabbed into his side brings out blood and water. Yes, he is dead, but soon his friends meet him by the same lake he once walked across.

To mark the end of selfish life and the start of spiritual life, new Christians are ceremoniously washed in water.

And so the water flows on.

Whenever you drink from a fountain or a bottle of Evian this week, make it a silent toast to this stream that runs through a book written for people who are 90 percent water themselves ... and who, most of the time, have to admit that they are all wet.

"Men will flee to caves in the rocks and to holes in the ground from dread of the LORD and the splendor of his majesty, when he rises to shake the earth." Isaiah 2:19

04.05.2003: Bible is so full of holes you can't ignore them

The Bible is full of holes, you know. Believers hear that a lot from skeptics, even from those who've only flipped through the book once or twice, laying it aside without digging in. But when a critic of the document makes that claim, don't deny it. Just agree and point out some of the notable holes in the Bible:

A hole was left in the roof of the Capernaum house through which a paralyzed man was lowered by friends trying to get face time with Jesus. (Mark 2)

A hole was dug in the ground by a man who buried his master's money because he was too lazy or neurotic to put it to use. Jesus' parable about this ends with the digger tossed out on his ear. (Matthew 25)

If you asked the mighty Philistines of David's youth, they'd have told you that the Hebrews were so scared they lived in holes in the ground. Soon, however, talking trash like that got 20 Philistines killed by Jonathan, and many more by his father's army. (1 Samuel 14)

Job cautioned that you can't catch a hippopotamus by the hole in his nose. (Job 40)

If you worry more about cash than about the riches of God, the prophet says you're putting your wages in a purse with a hole in it. (Haggai 1)

Playing charades so the smug inhabitants of Jerusalem would pay attention, Ezekiel made a hole in the city wall, then crawled out carrying his bags as a sign of doom on the way. (Ezekiel 12)

Joseph was tossed into a hole by his jealous brothers, and went from there to a hole of a prison. With a little extra attention from God, though, he ended up with a whole lot of blessings in Egypt. (Genesis 37)

And when Joseph's people were transplanted out of Egypt many years later, there were no holes in the clothing or the shoes of the Israelites, even though they never got within shopping range of a mall or a Wal-Mart as they roamed across the desert for 40 years. They may not have always acted like a holy people, but their God didn't let them get holey.

When one of those same Israelites left camp for a restroom break, they were commanded to take a shovel or something and dig a hole to promote hygiene. (Deuteronomy 23)

Jesus didn't even have a hole to call his own. He warned one man who was interested in following him that, "Foxes have holes and birds of the air have nests, but the Son of Man has no place to lay his head." (Matthew 8)

A few years after Jesus left the earth, some of his followers did have holes of their own. Persecuted for their beliefs, "They wandered in deserts and mountains, and in caves and holes in the ground." (Hebrews 11)

Another hole was left in Jesus' side big enough for Thomas to stick his fist into. (John 20)

But by far the biggest hole in the Bible was the tomb in which Jesus' dead body rested. There's always an echo in a hole, but when after three days that hole was empty again, the echo was heard around the world and across the centuries.

" 'Simon,' he said to Peter, 'are you asleep? Could you not keep watch for one hour? Watch and pray so that you will not fall into temptation'." Mark 14:37-38

03.27.2004: That drowsy trio finally woke up and got to work

Peter, James and John weren't bad guys. They weren't losers. At the very least they had potential, or Jesus would not have chosen them to keep him company while he poured out his soul at Gethsemane.

"Stay here and keep watch," he told them, but three times Jesus paused from his prayers and found Peter, James and John asleep. After he woke them up the second time, they didn't know what to say to him, St. Mark writes.

After their third nap, it was too late even to apologize. As they yawned, stretched and shook the fog from their brains, Judas was already walking up with the armed mob that would take Jesus away. Nor is it likely that they got any sleep for the rest of the night, even without Jesus there to shake them to alertness. Certainly at the first hint of dawn, when the rooster crowed, Peter was wider awake than he'd ever been in his life.

Jesus was not particularly hard on the tired trio – "The spirit is willing, but the flesh is weak," he said – so I want to give them the benefit of the doubt. But why did they sleep?

Some people say it was just the end of a rigorous week for the apostles, with the kind of fatigue you always feel after a few days on the road. That seems unlikely. Traipsing around Jerusalem would probably wear me out, but these were fishermen by trade, used to hard work, long hours and then more hard work.

Some people say the devil was at work, sending the three to sleep as just one more small way to inflict pain on the loneliest man in history. And maybe this would put a wedge between the divine leader and his all-too-human disciples. In particular, Jesus knew he was in a battle for Simon Peter's soul, as he told him flat out earlier in the evening: "Simon, Simon, Satan has asked to sift you as wheat." But, no, if their sleep came from a magic sweep of Satan's wand, surely Jesus would have told them so.

A likelier reason is that the apostles felt warm and secure under the Lord's leadership. He'd never let them down, never let them be lynched. He'd even shown them how to relax and nap at tense times – like in a small fishing boat during an awful storm.

So, in these quiet hours, in the eye of the tornado that would soon engulf them all, Peter, James and John were relaxed. Just a few yards from Jesus, they were content to let him carry on his shoulders all of the worries of the day. Not quite sure what he'd been talking about in the upper room, they bedded down like sheep near the shepherd.

And then he was gone.

They saw him arrested, saw him on the cross, saw him rise into the clouds.

And as he left, they awoke.

One evening, for example, Peter and John were tossed in jail for preaching about Jesus. This time it was the Jerusalem rulers who fell asleep, and by the time they woke up the next morning to punish Peter and John, 5,000 people had heard their message and believed it.

Once so drowsy, these men soon spread a wake-up call around the world. So is there hope for a sleeper like me?

*"The LORD will surely comfort Zion and will look with
compassion on all her ruins; he will make her deserts like Eden,
her wastelands like the garden of the LORD. Joy and gladness
will be found in her, thanksgiving and the sound of singing."*
                                                    Isaiah 51:3

06.22.2002: For some people, most important parts of life take place in a garden

One of the side benefits of gardening is that you have time for meditation, out there alone among the tomatoes, zucchini and crabgrass. Maybe you think about how your garden compares to some others.

Eden was built around a pair of trees. Gethsemane was just an olive grove on a hill. Joseph's Garden was a rich man's monument, planted around a tomb.

Eden was "pleasing to the eye and good for food," a double compliment for any gardener. God himself enjoyed a walk through Eden. Another of his perfect creations, man, strolled beside God, and they talked about the important matters of the world, of why things were and of how they would be.

In Gethsemane, too, a perfect man talked to God of why things were.

In Joseph's garden, God talked back, his action speaking louder than words could to every imperfect man.

Eden was watered by a mighty river that spread life far beyond the garden. Gethsemane was watered by the tears of a man with a mighty love ready to die to spread life. Joseph's garden was watered by the tears of a woman who feared that the one she loved mightily was dead.

The paradise of Eden was not eternal, and so one day there was a sword at its gate, a flaming one to warn away man. To enter meant death. Of course, life outside the garden was only a slower death.

The sword in Gethsemane, it served no real purpose. Peter swung wildly with it, but Jesus healed the wound and told him to put the sword away. Nor did the swords in Joseph's garden serve any real purpose in the guards' hands.

Not far from Eden was a corpse. Cain stood over it worried about punishment. It wasn't mankind's first sin, nor our last, but it was our first corpse.

Not far from Gethsemane was a corpse. Judas, realizing the consequences of his crime, punished himself. It wasn't mankind's first sin, but it was one of our greatest.

Not far from Joseph's garden was a corpse. Joseph waited until the punishment of Golgotha was over, then took the corpse away to his garden.

Then, in Joseph's garden tomb, there was no corpse. Mary Magdalene looked. John looked. Peter looked. The guards looked. But there was no corpse.

This made Mary cry, standing there at the tomb, until a man she thought was the gardener asked why she was crying. He said her name, and she realized it was Jesus, the one she'd been looking for. But there was still no corpse.

And maybe Mary Magdalene was right in thinking that she was talking to the gardener. His message to her that day was, "I am returning to my Father and your Father, to my God and your God."

Think about it: Eden, Gethsemane, Joseph's garden. And a fourth garden, watered by the river of life, beside which grows a tree transplanted from the center of Eden.

It took more than a green thumb to revive that tree. Gardeners like yourself can appreciate that as you meditate, out there among the tomatoes.

"When the centurion and those with him who were guarding
Jesus saw the earthquake and all that had happened, they were
terrified, and exclaimed, 'Surely he was the Son of God!' "
                                                    Matthew 27:54

04.06.2002: All the dead men walking were just a part of amazing chain of events

Easter Sunday was a climax for the Christian calendar, but the weeks after contain plenty of excitement, too.

For starters, St. Matthew informs us that when Jesus died, "The tombs broke open and the bodies of many holy people who had died were raised to life. They came out of the tombs, and after Jesus' resurrection they went into the holy city and appeared to many people."

No word on how long all those bodies hung around in Jerusalem. Were they crumbling zombies terrorizing the city, or fully restored people who walked into their old homes and asked what was for dinner?

I like to think that when Christ was resurrected a couple days later, they decided that being dead wasn't so scary after all, and marched happily back to the cemeteries. Maybe they even waved to friends and families. "Good-bye. See you soon. I'll save you a spot."

I like to think that.

If true it makes a great object lesson to us, the living, who want to stay out of the cemetery at any cost, even if we do claim to believe it is the gateway to wonderful things beyond.

Living with that sort of fear, seeing yourself as limited only to the crumbling, scary existence of Earth, can turn you into a zombie for sure.

Jesus himself, meanwhile, did not step out of the grave and immediately head for heaven like some harried frequent flier. St. Luke says he stayed on Earth for 40 days before going home to God.

Later on, St. Paul writes to some friends and lists the people who saw Jesus during this 40 days: "He appeared to Peter, and then to the Twelve.

"After that, he appeared to more than 500 of the brothers at the same time ... Then he appeared to James, then to all the apostles, and last of all he appeared to me also."

Forty days and 500 people were enough to reach critical mass, to establish the empty tomb and the living Jesus as indisputable facts. Enough to foil the cover-up started by the priests, who paid the guards to keep their mouths closed about what happened at the tomb.

But a bigger barrier to clear in establishing these facts was the doleful doubts of the apostles themselves. St. Mark writes that when Jesus rejoined his old gang, he lectured them "for their lack of faith and their stubborn refusal to believe those who had seen him after he had risen." So apparently it wasn't just Thomas who doubted.

Makes you wonder if the apostles waved away the first 499 people who told them stories of a resurrected Jesus, finally to be swayed by the 500th.

That would be the worst-case scenario, but even if it's true you still have to show respect for these guys. Once their doubts and objections were answered, they spread the story across and beyond the Roman Empire faster than a chain letter. Slow starters, but strong finishers.

That empire's long gone, but the story is still spreading.

Don't break the chain.

"Forgetting what is behind and straining toward what is ahead, I press on toward the goal to win the prize for which God has called me heavenward in Christ Jesus." Philippians 3:13-14

08.18.2001: Some very happy people have had a lot of rubbish in their lives

How sad if you never walk into a forest meadow, far off the marked trail, and have that cool, green feeling that you are the first person to see this spot, to walk on these mosses, to hear this silence.

How sad if you never look at the impossible task, heave a sigh and do it anyway. Split the cord of firewood in a single afternoon, or alter all of the bridesmaids' dresses the day before the wedding, or write the three term papers in time for a passing grade. And that night fall to sleep happy.

How sad if you never tingle to the cheers and backslaps of your friends and teammates as you come through for them in the last inning, frame, set, quarter, hand, point or mile and know that for an instant you are their Most Valuable Player.

How sad if you never get to hear the very first cry of your very own child, flesh of your flesh, and comfort that beautiful creation and promise that you will always be there to protect it from the things in the world that will make it cry many more times.

How sad if you never find a friend, and slowly build a bridge between your heart and hers that over the years becomes so strong that it is unshaken by distances and differences, so wide that it can carry load after load of secret thoughts in both directions at the same time, without fear of a crash or a spill.

How sad if you never follow a whim, a wild hair, and change your vacation plans in midroute, following a road sign that intrigues you but that isn't on the map, so that you end up with three rolls of serendipitous snapshots that you can't wait to show your friends.

How sad if you never sit intrigued at the feet of a good teacher, absorbed in what he is saying, asking occasional questions but mostly just learning, and thinking not at all about whether this stuff will be on the next test because you want to know it anyway.

How sad if you never get a surprise birthday party, or an unexpected commendation from the boss of your boss, or if they never call you to come blushingly out of your spot in the wings and say as the ovation begins, "Here's the guy who really made this all possible!"

How sad if you never become the most important person in another person's life and stay that way throughout it.

How sad if the greatest day of your life is behind you, and you're resigned to that and have given up trying to have another day as good.

And yet, how much sadder if you accomplish one, or some, or all 10 of these things and never come face to face with him who made them all possible.

This is what Paul the apostle meant when he wrote, "Whatever was to my profit I now consider loss for the sake of Christ. What is more, I consider everything a loss compared to the surpassing greatness of knowing Christ Jesus my Lord, for whose sake I have lost all things. I consider them rubbish, that I may gain Christ and be found in him."

"Do not repay anyone evil for evil. Be careful to do what is right in the eyes of everybody. If it is possible, as far as it depends on you, live at peace with everyone." Romans 12:17-18

11.02.2002: How 2 great men ended their battle of unkind words about unkind cuts

Face to face, Theologian One told Theologian Two that he was completely off base. Then he wrote a detailed letter explaining why.

Copies went everywhere. Theologian One did not mince words about what those who led Theologian Two down the wrong path could do with their stupid doctrine. To make matters worse, the letter was included in a compilation of similar essays.

It became a bestseller. And you know how it is with TV shows and movies and the like – people always talk about the most outrageous bits. Why else does Jerry Springer thrive?

This whole fracas actually took place a long time ago, before reality TV or talk radio.

Theologian One was the Apostle Paul. Theologian Two was the Apostle Peter. Between them, these two giants penned much of the New Testament.

Here's the two-minute recap of their big disagreement:

Peter, napping on an empty stomach, has a vision of a bunch of non-kosher animals and hears the Lord tell him to kill one and eat.

"No way," he says.

"Yes way," says the Lord. Peter wakes up to find that a gentile is summoning him – he wants to hear about Jesus. Peter takes the hint that the Christian message is for the whole world and has nothing to do with being Jewish. The other apostles agree that this is a wonderful thing.

Meanwhile, Paul converts from Judaism to Christianity and starts preaching to gentiles. After three years he goes on a retreat to Jerusalem to meet Peter. They impress each other, then get back to work.

Paul has a lot of work to do, because some Jewish Christians are following him around, telling his converts that to be right with God they need to be circumcised.

This infuriates Paul, and he fights against it for years.

Then he finds out that Peter is refusing to eat with believers unless they've been circumcised.

That does it. Paul writes that the first time he saw Peter "I opposed him to his face" for this hypocrisy.

Read Galatians for the complete argument against men needing to cut a piece of skin from their genitals to get right with God. The stunner in this discourse, showing the depth of Paul's anger, is this verse: "As for those agitators, I wish they would go the whole way and emasculate themselves!"

Ouch.

But there is a lesson in this war of words. Paul and Peter were imperfect men, but what made them great was their unrelenting focus on the one they followed. It got them past this argument, healing a wound that threatened to split one movement into two.

Almost the last words Peter wrote hint at this healing: "Our Lord's patience means salvation, just as our dear brother Paul also wrote you with the wisdom that God gave him. ... His letters contain some things that are hard to understand, which ignorant and unstable people distort, as they do the other Scriptures, to their own destruction."

Wish I could speak so kindly about the folks I disagree with.

SECTION FOUR:
IT'S ALL ABOUT JESUS

"And the child grew and became strong; he was filled with wisdom, and the grace of God was upon him." Luke 2:40

09.01.2001: One trip changes a lot of things when you're 12 years old

You know what 12-year-old boys are like. They bounce back and forth a lot. They play with kids' toys one minute and imitate teen-agers the next. Big changes come when you're 12.

So you'll understand what the trip was like. Part of the time he was being responsible, helping his parents with the bags, keeping his little half brothers in line. You know what blended families are like.

But streams of families were on the same road and in the same camping spots, so part of the time he was off with other 12-year-olds engaged in a lot of bouncing back and forth.

He was a good kid. The adults mostly ignored the shifting gaggle of children in the caravan, but every once in a while you might see a mother smile at him, or chide her own 12-year-old, "Why can't you be more like Jesus?"

He had mixed emotions when they got to Jerusalem.

Getting there was the point of the trip, after all, but it meant he had to wave goodbye to his new friends and hope they could play again on the way home, after the Feast.

The family did the Feast thing like proper pilgrims and tourists. Jesus had plenty of time for what he'd awaited since they left Nazareth.

He went to the outdoor classrooms of the day's top preacher/teachers. He stayed on the edges of the crowd at first; you know how the presence of important men like these makes adults frown at children. But every time he opened his mouth to ask a question or answer one, Jesus found himself closer to the center of attention.

He amazed the scholars and the students and the tourists and the groupies hanging around the courts. He lost track of the days and became immersed in the words of God, explaining and loving each one. If one of the 12-year-old buddies from the trip had wandered through and waved at him, Jesus wouldn't have seen him. He was doing what he was born to do.

He could see wrinkles on the foreheads of some of the teachers, an odd darkness in the eyes that grew with the amazement of the crowd for Jesus' words. Mostly, though, it was a wonderful time.

And then, suddenly, it was over. Joseph and Mary were calling him away. "Son, why have you treated us like this?" his mother asked. "Your father and I have been anxiously searching for you." They'd actually left Jerusalem and gotten a day away without him, thinking Jesus must be off playing with the other 12s.

Alight with the study and teaching he'd been doing, he asked Mary – but not with the "Duh!" of today's 12-year-olds: "Didn't you know I had to be in my Father's house?"

They didn't know what he was talking about, and there were a lot of footsteps back to Nazareth. At least three days behind schedule, walking took precedence over discussion.

But the other 12-year-olds noticed that Jesus wasn't as eager to play now. He seemed quieter, older, more apart.

He loved Jerusalem, and he knew he'd go back some day.

"Anyone who loves his father or mother more than me is not worthy of me; anyone who loves his son or daughter more than me is not worthy of me; and anyone who does not take his cross and follow me is not worthy of me." Matthew 10:37-38

07.13.2002: Afraid your family will think you're crazy if you act the way Jesus did?

Oh, sure, now that he's gone on to be famous, everybody wants a piece of Jesus. Brothers, cousins, uncles.

Anyone with a drop of Mary or Joseph's blood wants to talk about how they're related to Jesus.

Some of these characters are just pretentious pretenders, but maybe it's Jesus' real relatives who ought to be ashamed of themselves.

They claim him now, but what they forget to tell you is that they came within a hair of having Jesus declared insane before he even got his ministry organized.

Mark writes a bit about this. It's early on in Jesus' adulthood – he's only preached a few times in Galilee's little synagogues and hills, healed a few sick people and made a couple provocative statements about being "the Son of Man," whatever that means. The family always knew he was odd, but when he was just a kid it hadn't really been a problem. All grown up, though, Jesus made a scene.

When he picked out those 12 men to follow him, he took them into someone's house for a first meal together. The house was mobbed by so many people that Jesus and the others couldn't even eat.

Everyone was talking about him, and Jesus' relatives had had enough embarrassment.

Mark says, "When his family heard about this, they went to take charge of him, for they said, 'He is out of his mind.'"

Of course, they were just a simple country family, so when they got to Jesus they found a second opinion about him from some big-city professionals.

Mark says the professionals pretty much concurred with the family's diagnosis:

"And the teachers of the law who came down from Jerusalem said, 'He is possessed by Beelzebub! By the prince of demons he is driving out demons.'"

About then Mary showed up with Jesus' brothers. They stood outside and sent someone in to fetch Jesus, but he wouldn't come out. "Who are my mother and my brothers?" he asked. Then he looked at those seated in a circle around him and said, "Here are my mother and my brothers!"

Maybe they all had a good laugh, while his brothers fumed outside, but Jesus was serious. He never went home again. He lived on the road, off the kindness of strangers. His reputation for strangeness – and greatness – grew, until pretty soon those professionals down in Jerusalem were asking Jesus for his opinion.

Eventually most of the family came around, decided he wasn't crazy. As a matter of fact, one thing that helped Jesus get through the last couple hours before his death was seeing his mother down there below the cross, knowing that she knew who he was.

The same family tension still happens today, you know. A lot of people feel pulled to crank up their Christian life from a sleepy level to something approaching fanaticism. Their fear, though, is that the family will think they're crazy. It's not an irrational fear, but it can be a powerful one. Do what you can to exorcise that fear from your house.

"Blessed are those who hunger and thirst for
righteousness, for they will be filled." Matthew 5:6

08.26.2000: Jesus fed the masses,
but how many left hungry?

One of the slanders brought against early Christians was cannibalism. You can see how their persecutors arrived at that conclusion, when the believers talked so much about eating the body and drinking the blood of their executed leader.

This was hardly the first time two sides looked at the communion meal and arrived at different conclusions. Poke your head inside a few church buildings this weekend and you'll see the bread and wine administered across a spectrum of ceremonies, frequencies, tastes and trappings.

And it is still one of the mysteries of Christianity, this rough meal that stands for so much, and that has stood for so long.

Before Jesus ever ate the Last Supper that turned into today's ceremonies, he fixed another meal and passed it out to the hungry. With 5,000 men and their families to feed, there must have been a spectrum of tastes and trappings among the crowd that day, too.

And you have to wonder what the reaction was after Jesus turned a boy's lunchbox of bread and fish into enough food to satisfy the crowd.

Do you suppose there were people in the mob who saved their portion, who nibbled at one corner but then wrapped the rest in a napkin and took it home?

"Let me show you the miracle food," they'd say to every visitor for years to come. "I was there that day. I saw the whole thing." Maybe they ate a crumb every day, trying to make it last a lifetime. And would the meal stay miraculously fresh, locked away in a drawer, or would it smell like … rotten fish?

Do you suppose there were those who ate more than their fair share, who still had a mouth and two hands full of fish sandwiches while the apostles were trying to clean up? Did they get stomachaches later?

Do you suppose there were enemies of Jesus, sprinkled in the crowd to spy on him, who refused to eat the miraculous meal, even though they could smell it and see how much the guys in front of them were enjoying it?

Do you suppose many people said thank you after they'd eaten?

Do you suppose anybody asked for the recipe? Maybe the mother of the boy who volunteered his lunch became as famous as Sister Schubert for her bakery.

What a day. I wonder what that hillside scene was like. I wonder also what happened to all of the people who ate the meal Jesus blessed.

Out of 5,000, how many stuck around a few years later to eat of the communion meal, to celebrate and remember the risen Christ?

How many forgot about him, forgot about the loaves and fishes, and went on looking for someone else to satisfy their hungers?

You might think about that the next time you're sharing the holy communion. About how sad it would be to be given a fresh meal, straight from the hands of God, and not realize what you had.

Savor the taste.

"And when the day of Pentecost was fully come, they were all with one accord in one place." Acts 2:1 (KJV)

07.15.2000: WWJD? To be more specific:
What Would Jesus Drive?

You mosey along I-565, visor down because the sun is at a vicious angle, and catch the bumper sticker on that silvery Lexus passing to your left. You tend to notice shiny Lexi; wouldn't mind having one yourself.

You've seen the same sticker on all kinds of cars, but it's thought-provoking on a Lexus: W.W.J.D.

Interesting question. One you can slowly turn over in your mind, because you're going to be on this road a few more miles.

What Would Jesus Do?

Well, what would Jesus drive?

Let's give the guy in the Lexus the benefit of the doubt, and say that he's driving exactly the model Jesus would choose if he lived in 21st-century Alabama.

We have to suppose that Jesus has chosen a short-term lease, rather than buying the car outright, because he's not planning to be around long enough to make 60 payments.

But a bigger problem is where to put the apostles. An 11-passenger van might be better than the Lexus. The Twelve can fit in with Jesus, if Andrew sits on his brother's lap and they stuff James the Less into the cargo space.

Or maybe two vehicles – the van for mission trips and the Lexus for when Jesus needs to be alone with his father. Better change that Lexus to a Jeep Cherokee, though, because Jesus' favorite spot for solitude is in the mountains.

Maybe you imagine Jesus in a secondhand Ford station wagon with bald tires, a leaky transmission and three colors of paint, which Judas selected because it was the cheapest thing on the lot. The exhaust is smoky, but thanks to prayer the thing keeps running.

On the other hand, there's always public transportation, which gets you around the city pretty well, and Greyhound for longer trips. But that's mostly for unfortunates with no car of their own. Can you see the King of Kings sitting with some of the people you meet on a city bus?

Jesus might even be a hitchhiker, though these days most of his followers think it's too dangerous to pick up strangers by the roadside. Best just to pass by in the far lane; raise a trooper on the cell phone if the guy looks suspicious.

Sure, transportation is more complicated these days. But even way back in Palestine, there were chariots, donkeys, horses, camels. For some reason, Jesus only caught a ride on special occasions like his Triumphal Entry, which was really more of a parade than a way to get across Jerusalem.

Most of the time Jesus just walked. He sweated. He got pebbles in his sandals. It took forever to get anyplace – and you think you have a lot to accomplish in a short time.

He met a lot of fellow pedestrians along those dirt roads, and they were sweaty, too, and sometimes diseased, and sometimes weird, and mostly just not the kind of people you'd invite into your Lexus without spreading a towel on the seat first.

So what would Jesus drive?

That's a tough one.

As you decide what kind of car to put your bumper stickers on, another good question would be, "What drives you?"

"Jesus replied, 'Foxes have holes and birds of the air have nests, but the Son of Man has no place to lay his head.' "
Matthew 8:20

09.04.2004: This time, WWJD asks a dreamy question

Our question today is – not for the first time: WWJD? What would Jesus dream?

I don't mean the sort of dream Martin Luther King Jr. talked of – a goal or hope. I mean the sort of dream you had last night when your head hit the pillow, your breathing slowed, your eyelids fluttered.

Actually, Jesus said he had nowhere to rest his head, so the pillow part doesn't apply. But he had to sleep sometimes, and when he did, I wonder what he dreamed?

The answer rests, I suppose, on the question of where dreams come from.

Do dreams mean more than I'll ever know, as Freud hypothesized? Or are they just biological flickerings – a random response of the cerebral cortex, immediately forgotten?

Are they tiny visions sent from God, glimpses of the eternal? That's what Chris Rice imagined in his beautiful song "Deep Enough to Dream," about a lazy summer nap:

"Deep enough to dream in brilliant colors I have never seen.
Deep enough to join a billion people for a wedding feast.
Deep enough to reach out and touch the face of the One who made me.
And oh, the love I feel, and oh the peace. Do I ever have to wake up?"

Or are dreams sent from the underworld in an attempt to take control of our lives, as those "Nightmare on Elm Street" movies imagined?

If that's the case, I feel sorry for that monk of a millennium ago, locked in his desert cell, having renounced all worldly pleasures and comforts in an attempt to free himself from Satan. He eats his meager supper, says his prayers and falls asleep …

perchance to dream of something so ungodly that the next morning he must punish himself more severely.

From a spiritual perspective, dreams are like a 24-theater cineplex, playing an evershifting assortment of movies with MPAA ratings from G to X. By day, when I'm awake, I know that there are certain theaters I should not enter.

By night, though, I don't seem to have control over what sort of dreams fill my head. Maybe there's a loose link between the life I lead and the dreams I see, but surely there also are nights when Charles Manson dreams of butterflies and Billy Graham dreams of being chased by werewolves.

So what of Jesus Christ? If he was 100 percent human, surely he was a dreamer. What pictures flashed through his mind as he dozed by some roadside with a dozen friends scattered around him?

I wonder, in particular, about two things.

First, I wonder how often he dreamed of the cross. I wonder how many nights for Jesus were like a 24-theater cineplex where every screen was showing "Passion of the Christ." I wonder if nights like that led him into solitary days of prayer.

Second, I wonder if he ever dreamed about me. And if so, were those dreams comforting or disturbing?

I wonder about things like this by day. I also wonder why Jesus does not fill my dreams by night.

I'll have to sleep on that.

"And if I go and prepare a place for you, I will come back and
take you to be with me that you also may be where I am."
John 14:3

09.20.2003: The builder's doing a great job on my home

Once upon a time I wanted to be an architect. I even studied the subject throughout high school. I learned that square rooms are cheaper than round ones, that hallways are wasted footage and that I was better suited to a career where you didn't have to sharpen your pencil quite so much.

So I've lost touch with the architectural world.

I've never even had a house built specifically for me. I've always lived in places designed for other folks, who got to decide how many electrical outlets were needed and whether the garage could hold a car and a lawnmower at the same time.

I did build a treehouse for my two youngest boys last summer, a process of tough compromise between the height of their dreams, the depth of my wallet and the breadth of my woodworking skills. It is still standing.

And I have had a number of friends tell me how exhausted they were by the time they finally moved into a new home – worn out by watching the contractor every day to be sure he built it the way they wanted it.

And I've had contractors tell me how exhausting it is when customers change their minds every day about the size of the laundry room or the color of the cabinets.

All of which makes it very comforting to me that I have a master craftsman at work right now designing a custom home for me. He's the most trustworthy guy I'll ever meet, so I don't have to worry about checking on his progress all the time. The whole place is going to be a complete surprise when I finally move in. It wasn't even my idea, really, he just sent me a message that said, "In my father's house are many mansions – I am going there to prepare a place for you."

I haven't seen the lot, but I know it's riverfront property. The scenery is supposed to be gorgeous – the biggest tree in the neighborhood is one of a kind, he tells me, with a different fruit every month.

My builder also doesn't mind changing the floor plan as he goes. In fact, he keeps an eye on my lifestyle and my priorities and if they change he just goes back to the drawing board to come up with a new plan that's perfect for me. There's not a contractor on Earth who'll treat you like that.

For example, the library keeps getting bigger and bigger as I discover more and more books I wish I had time to read. A lot of them are about him and his father.

One of the things I haven't figured out is how he keeps expanding my home when all around it are places just as flexible that he's building for other people.

This has got to be expensive, because the real estate where he's building is so precious it might as well be paved with gold, but my builder says it's within our budget. "If it were not so, I would have told you," he says.

I believe him, but I can't help thinking that somebody's going to have to pay dearly for the mansion he's preparing for me.

I suspect it's him.

*"Not everyone who says to me, 'Lord, Lord,' will enter the
kingdom of heaven." Matthew 7:21*

09.27.2003: Maybe Jesus needs to get
a no-call list of his own

Fifty million people in this country have spoken up to say
they don't want telemarketers to call them anymore. The rest are
just waiting for some vacation salesman to pause for breath so
they can shout, "No!" and hang up.

Personally, I avoid most of these calls by letting my wife
answer the phone – even if she's already holding the baby, the
cheese grater and a basket of dirty soccer uniforms. The calls are
all for her anyway.

Yet, amazingly, she is the only American I know who does
not have a cell phone, because she realizes that owning one
would exponentially increase her telephone time. I honestly
admire her for resisting the temptation, but I don't expect she can
hold out much longer.

But anyway, if she's not home and I do get stuck taking a call
from some stranger who cannot pronounce my name but wants to
tell me why I should refinance my home or take the family to
Florida, I've found the best defense is honesty.

"Right now I'm watching 'Bambi' with my 6-year-old," I'll
tell the caller.

Or, "My whole family is actually sitting down to dinner
together."

Then I'll ask, "Is your call more important than that?"

The response surprised me at first, but I'm now pretty
confident that even a rabid telemarketers will hesitate for a
moment, admit, "No, it's not" and hang up.

I like to think that this makes the guy stop and think about his
priorities, maybe even that he quits his job and finds a new one
that's more noble. I have a bad habit of misjudging my impact on
people.

But hold the phone. I'm getting off track here.

What I wanted to say is that maybe Jesus ought to look into establishing a no-call list of his own.

Now, heaven is set up sort of the opposite of my house, so that even though Jesus knows all of the calls are for God, he's always the one who picks up the phone.

And the way I picture it, Jesus puts his hand over the receiver and says, "It's for you, Father. It's a friend of mine calling to ask you something."

And God says something like, "I'm busy watching the angels on parade right now. Is this call more important?"

And Jesus says, "Yes, it is."

And God smiles and says, "Right. I'll take it."

Then Jesus puts the call on the speaker phone so the Holy Spirit can hear it, too.

Or something like that.

But the point is, maybe Jesus could set up a list of all of the people who don't call him. And maybe he could take a legion of those parading angels and retrain them into telemarketers. And maybe he could give them his no-call list and tell the angels to ring everyone on it and ask, nicely, what happened to their prayer life.

Maybe he could, but in a country where millions of people don't want to be bothered, it seems unlikely. I guess he'll just sit by the phone, instead, wishing more strangers would call.

SECTION FIVE:
TODAY'S HEADLINES

*"Enter through the narrow gate. For wide is the gate and broad
is the road that leads to destruction, and many enter through it.
But small is the gate and narrow the road that leads to life,
and only a few find it." Matthew 7:13-14*

04.07.2001: They do add up, those sad, little crosses beside the highway

If the custom catches on, we might all become too frightened to drive.

Or at least we will slow down a little.

As it is, the wooden crosses you see occasionally just off the shoulder of the highway are saddening. Most of them are simple, maybe 2 feet tall, with a cluster of artificial flowers, a flapping ribbon and the name of another son or daughter or spouse killed in a car wreck.

Many are homemade, deeply personal expressions of grief and remembrance. You don't see them in every community; maybe there are local laws against unauthorized signs on the roadway, or maybe it's just a Southern thing to enshrine the spot where a loved one suddenly turned into a statistic.

And those statistics are frightening. Every year for the past several decades, around 40,000 loved ones in the United States have been killed in crashes. Most years in Alabama it's a little more than a thousand fatalities.

Imagine what driving would be like if every time the U.S. Department of Transportation made another tally mark in its grim statistics book, the mark was represented by a new little cross stuck into the gravel or grass along some roadway. Add a thousand crosses a year to Alabama roads and in less than a decade you would never look up from behind the steering wheel without seeing one.

Somebody fell asleep by that bridge.

A drunk driver was the only survivor in three cars at that intersection.

A teen-ager's life ended on that little curve back there.

What would driving be like under that constant, inescapable reminder of the potential danger of what you were doing? Another year, another 40,000 little crosses, and the reminder grows thicker and harder to ignore.

Would you stop driving altogether? Would you spend more money on a stouter SUV or a sturdier Volvo? Would you go into denial, insisting it could never happen to you?

Don't fret. It's not likely to happen.

By the time the road toll of 2002 begins to accumulate, the wreck victims of 2001 will be remembered only by inner circles of family and friends. More crash-test commercials and buckle-up billboards will have to be ordered to keep drivers from getting cocky. Getting there fast will still be the top American priority.

So don't fret.

Instead, fret for a minute about a scarier scenario.

What if a little marker went up every time you made a mistake in life, drove off the straight 'n' narrow, went too fast and flipped, or just fell asleep for an instant and hit an abutment? And what if God kept track of those statistics?

And what if you could see them all in your rear-view mirror, where objects are closer than they appear?

What would the road of life be like under that constant, inescapable reminder of the certain destruction you were driving toward?

If that were the scenario, would you go into denial?

Or maybe let Jesus drive.

"So the LORD scattered them from there over all the earth, and they stopped building the city. That is why it was called Babel – because there the LORD confused the language of the whole world. From there the LORD scattered them over the face of the whole earth." Genesis 11:8-9

09.15.2001: So much of our pain springs from the broken base of that tower

The broken base of a once-proud tower may still rest there, buried in the dust of time. So much of our history can be traced to that tower, so much sadness and suffering and hatred. So many misunderstood words.

Babel was built on the plain of Shinar, when men discovered how to bake bricks and looked around for a project worthy of their new skill. The arrogant builders said, "Come, let us build ourselves a city, with a tower that reaches to the heavens, so that we may make a name for ourselves and not be scattered over the face of the whole earth."

The Bible doesn't say how far along they had gotten on the tower and the city before God stopped the project. Maybe it was 110 stories, maybe just a few bricks that are still out there somewhere, buried lumps of clay – unrecognizable for what they once represented.

"If as one people speaking the same language they have begun to do this, then nothing they plan to do will be impossible for them," said the Lord when he surveyed their plans. "Come, let us go down and confuse their language so they will not understand each other."

Was God unnecessarily harsh on the people, splintering them into tribes that couldn't communicate? That is for God to decide, but compared to his previous punishment – the flood – maybe Babel was just a slap on the wrist. Harsh or not, it was effective.

But the world hasn't changed much since Babel, has it?

We still can't talk to each other. The language barrier can be broken, but the very pride that makes us think we can stack bricks to the heavens keeps us from open, humble communication.

So nations quarrel with nations and neighbors with neighbors. To this day the constant babble has kept the world from accomplishing much of anything.

In New York City, the broken base of a once-proud tower is the latest example. Men who could not talk to other men decided to let death and destruction speak for them.

I am not saying that the World Trade Center was another Babel, another tower that never should have been built and so was struck down by God's hand. But I am saying that without Babel there would be no World Trade Center collapse, no Pentagon explosion, no blast at the Murrah Building and no bombs in our embassies or our Marine barracks. These and a thousand other atrocities are the heritage of Babel, which showed that man does not work well with others.

What can you do when you live in a world that speaks in quarrelsome, misunderstood sentences punctuated with explosions?

The only shot we have at getting back together and overcoming the curse of Babel may be Jesus, who once said, "I, when I am lifted up from the earth, will draw all men to myself."

If we're lifted up as high as he is, we won't need a tower.

"I will put my laws in their minds and write them on their hearts. I will be their God, and they will be my people. No longer will a man teach his neighbor, or a man his brother, saying, 'Know the Lord,' because they will all know me."
Hebrews 8:10-11

11.24.2001: Here's how Alabama could get more out of Ten Commandments

To make Alabama government efficient for a change, here's how to get maximum benefit from the Ten Commandments.

1. On Jan. 1, each adult resident gets an attractive badge, designed by the same folks who do our license plates.

This badge displays a big "10," and below in smaller print is the text of the Ten Commandments. You must wear your badge in plain view.

2. All law enforcement officials make the Ten Commandments their top priority. Violent crimes such as murder and robbery are obviously still covered. The commands against breaking the Sabbath and against coveting are tougher to enforce, but I predict that within a couple of months most folks will get the hang of it they'll show up every week for church services and they'll learn to keep their hands and eyes to themselves when they walk past a beautiful woman or home or car.

3. If you are convicted of breaking a commandment, you must trade in your badge for one with a big "9" and your offense highlighted on the text below.

Each time you break a commandment, you get a new badge with a lower number and more highlighting.

4. This will create a new class of commandment attorneys, dedicated to showing that their clients did not really covet or make a graven image or whatever. There will not, however, be as many loopholes for these lawyers to exploit as there are today. And if they aren't careful, both attorney and client in a losing case might be convicted of bearing false witness.

That first conviction results in a stiff fine.

Break two commandments and you go into work release.

Break three and the sentence is longer.

Break four and it's prison.

Break five within a year and you are considered beyond salvation. You are transferred to death row, where your execution is carried out by other inmates who already have broken the commandment against killing. (If it turns out God is against capital punishment, these guys have nothing to lose.)

5. Each Jan. 1, everyone gets a new "10" badge. Happy New Year.

6. Teens will get smaller "training" badges, but no penalties will be assessed for their infractions.

As another side benefit, everyone in the state will know how everyone else stands. You won't have to associate with riffraff. It'll be easier to decide whom to vote for.

Society will be transformed.

As another side benefit, this system will have people flocking to Jesus.

That's because after a couple of months, they'll read Galatians with a new interest and understanding.

Especially the part that says, "We were held prisoners by the law, locked up until faith should be revealed. So the law was put in charge to lead us to Christ that we might be justified by faith. Now that faith has come, we are no longer under the supervision of the law."

I can hardly wait to start.

"Marshal your troops, O city of troops, for a siege is laid against us. They will strike Israel's ruler on the cheek with a rod. But you, Bethlehem Ephrathah, though you are small among the clans of Judah, out of you will come for me one who will be ruler over Israel, whose origins are from of old, from ancient times." Micah 5:1

05.04.2002: Even if singing about Bethlehem seems pointless, we can't give up

O little town of Bethlehem,
How still we see thee lie;
Above thy deep and dreamless sleep
The silent stars go by;
Yet in thy dark streets shineth
The everlasting light.
The hopes and fears of all the years
Are met in thee tonight.
For Christ is born of Mary,
And gathered all above,
While mortals sleep the angels keep
Their watch of wond'ring love.
O morning stars, together
Proclaim the holy birth!
And praises sing to God the King,
And peace to men on earth!

It is far from Christmas in Bethlehem. Even if it were Christmas Eve, that sweet carol would sound sour with Palestinian gunmen and an assortment of civilians huddled in the Church of the Nativity.

Maybe, though, the author of the carol would think this a perfect time to sing it, softly and with feeling.

Bishop Phillips Brooks wrote the words above in 1868. He'd been to the Holy Land three years earlier, in 1865 when in America the smell of smoke still lingered from Civil War battlefields. Brooks was enchanted by the view of Bethlehem from the hills of Palestine at night. He had his church organist set his lyrics to music for their children's choir.

Ironically to today's situation it was written in Philadelphia, the city of brotherly love.

Of course, Sunday is not Christmas . . . in fact it is Easter on the Greek Orthodox calendar. The smell of smoke will be a lingering part of any Easter celebration managed within the Orthodox part of the church; three people were burned Thursday trying to put out a fire started there during the daily gun battle.

For 1,600 years various rulers have threatened to raze the Church of the Nativity, but this is its worst scarring since its dedication in 339.

There is no reason to believe that when the current standoff ends, peace will return to the city. Or to the rest of the Middle East. Or to the world.

When Arafat and Sharon and Powell and Bush and other names tied to the current conflict are sleeping a deep and dreamless sleep, other names will contend with other conflicts around the world.

The cycle will go on until, on some future day, not Christmas, not Easter, but a third great day, the most famous son of Bethlehem returns.

Until then ...

O riddled town of Bethlehem,
How shrill we see thee lie.
Despite retreats from ruined streets
Thy tensions multiply;
And in thy dark church shineth
No sniper-aiding light.
The pain and tears of all the years
Are met in thee tonight.
Where Christ was born of Mary
Are gathered men with guns
While mothers cry as children die
The silent stars watch stunned

O morning stars, together
Proclaim the standoff o'er!
And loudly cry that we must try
For peace midst men once more!

"Though one may be overpowered, two can defend themselves.
A cord of three strands is not quickly broken." Ecclesiastes 4:12

10.18.2003: What do you do about all these little numbers?

No special mathematical skill or NASA training is needed to answer this question: Any idea what the numbers below mean?

1 0 1 1 0 0 0 1 4 1 0 2 2 1 0 1 0 2 6 0 1 0 0 0 1 6 2 2 0 3 0
0 0 1 0 1 2 1 1 0 1 0 1 1 0 1 2 2 2 1 0 0 1 0 1 4 2 1 1 0 0 0
1 1 2 0 0 2 2 2 4 0 1 1 2 1 1 1 2 1 1 3 1 1 2 4 0 4 1 2 0 1 2
1 0 0 0 2 4 1 2 2 1 0 4 1 1 0 0 0 1 0 2 2 0 2 0 2 0 3 0 1 1 0
3 1 0 0 0 0 1 0 1 1 1 2 0 1 2 0 0 4 0 3 0 1 1 1 3 0 0 0 4 0
3 0 1 1 0 3 0 0 3 0 0

Answer: That's the number of U.S. service members killed each day in Iraq since May 1, when President Bush declared major combat operations complete. As I write, more than 300 U.S. soldiers, sailors, airmen and Marines have died in that country. It's a sad tally that continues to slowly add up, each new mark bringing tears to another family.

A little more than a month ago, the number of deaths in the actual, full-scale invasion of Iraq was surpassed by the number of deaths since May 1 – deaths from snipers, suicide bombers, Hummer wrecks, illnesses and other things.

Most of these deaths came one at a time. Most made neither the front page of the newspaper nor the world wrap-up on nightly

TV news. People care, but it's hard to get worked up anew for each tally mark.

I did not share this depressing list of little numbers to convince you the war in Iraq is wrong, or being mishandled, or is too terrible for America to finish. Patriots on both sides of that debate grieve these losses.

Rather, I am struck by the single digits as a way to remind you of a bit of scripture that you may already have heard before. It's Peter saying, "Be self-controlled and alert. Your enemy the devil prowls around like a roaring lion looking for someone to devour."

The way I see it, maybe you were in a brief, full-scale war with the devil whenever you first decided he was the enemy. And maybe that war went well, so that now you consider yourself a victor.

And maybe that war was hell on you. Maybe it cost you dearly to stand up that first time against the forces of evil.

However that big battle for your soul went down, remember that the toughest part of the Christian life is walking this Earth now, day after day, while the devil prowls around, lining up his next pot shot.

He specializes in this slow, ever-shifting warfare. He prowls, looking for a new way to hit you where it hurts. If you concentrate on controlling your temper, he'll attack you via some hot new Internet site. If you're careful to be generous and kind, he'll move the battle to a question of whether God's existence can be proved. If you make more time to cherish your family, he'll strike through a painful illness.

Slowly, he will continue to snipe away at you, maybe for the rest of your life. Your losses will add up. You will wonder whether it is worth the fight.

Don't be afraid. You can win! But be alert out there, and be sure you've got buddies to watch your back.

"And now I will show you the most excellent way. If I speak in the tongues of men and of angels, but have not love, I am only a resounding gong or a clanging cymbal."
1 Corinthians 12:31 – 13:1

06.28.2003: Show them how to find some real fireworks

Business is sizzling at the fireworks booths just outside the city limits. Their season flashes past like the bloom of an arctic flower. Already you're seeing HUGE sales here in the final week before the Fourth of July. Buy one, get FIVE free.

No one much wants fireworks on the fifth of July. Even budget-conscious housewives don't snatch them up the way they do Christmas wrapping paper on Dec. 26. You don't put M-80s and sparklers and Roman candles away for later, up on the top shelf somewhere.

Fireworks are about right now, about an extravagant display that shocks and awes. Instant thrills and chills and warm feelings spreading from your heart to the hairs on your neck. I don't know who invented the metaphor of fireworks for sex – it might have been that '70s TV show "Love American Style" – but it gets a lot of use for obvious reasons.

Plus, fireworks are both patriotic and religious – they help show your devotion to the God who delivered your forefathers from the British. John Adams said so, or sort of.

So this is a good time to talk about America and God and what the differences are between the two and what it means that the U.S. Supreme Court a few days ago ruled that states cannot make a law against two adults engaging in fireworks of one sort or another in the privacy of their own bedroom.

The objections made to this legalization of sodomy are mostly religious. Many godly people are upset that such behavior must be tolerated by the judicial system when it's decried in scripture.

If you are such an upset person, it might help to think of the situation this way.

Draw the United States of America as a circle – forget about Texas, Florida and the other pointy parts. Within this American community, draw a smaller circle to represent God's community.

In that outer circle, men make laws for order and safety, to give everybody the same decent shot at being a decent member of society.

In the inner circle, God makes laws; men try to follow them. They may not succeed fully in interpretation or application, but they try and pray and try some more, because they want to be where God is … because he is God.

People in the inner circle don't get to apply inner-circle law to outer-circle people. A lot times this is because the outer circle won't stand for it. "America is a free country," they say. "You can't legislate morality," they say. True, true.

And isn't it a waste of time to force inner-circle laws on people who don't want to come into the inner circle?

Instead, demonstrate that the inner circle is where the real fireworks are. Ones that don't fizzle after a few seconds. From a stand that won't be bankrupt in a few weeks.

Personally, I believe that the inner-circle people have what it takes to show off their "more excellent way." Problem is, too often they leave it on a top shelf somewhere, like a Roman candle they're thinking about saving until later.

But faith and fireworks are about right now.

SECTION SIX:
THE SPORTS REPORT

"The workers who were hired about the eleventh hour came and each received a denarius. So when those came who were hired first, they expected to receive more. But each one of them also received a denarius. When they received it, they began to grumble against the landowner. 'These men who were hired last worked only one hour,' they said, 'and you have made them equal to us who have borne the burden of the work and the heat of the day.' But he answered one of them, 'Friend, I am not being unfair to you. Didn't you agree to work for a denarius? Take your pay and go. I want to give the man who was hired last the same as I gave you. Don't I have the right to do what I want with my own money? Or are you envious because I am generous?' " Matthew 20:9-15

08.19.2000: Will the crowds spoil my personal relationship with the Rams?

As a kid in a bedraggled cotton town in central California, I saved my Cheerios box tops and sent off for a genuine pack of NFL playing cards.

I mailed the envelope with two convictions. One, that this was a venture best handled quietly. Dad was a preacher, and the propriety of playing cards was still a mite shaky in our circle.

Two, that I must have the Los Angeles Rams deck, with Roman Gabriel on the back of each card. This was when the Rams were still in Los Angeles, where they belonged. Before yellow or gold marred their uniforms. Before Roman Gabriel became a John Wayne sidekick.

When the deck finally arrived, I invented a convoluted football card game and shuffled my way through an entire mock playoff season. Incredibly, the Rams won my mock Super Bowl.

Fast-forward to 1978.

In the greatest movie ever made, "Heaven Can Wait," the Rams win the Super Bowl, as God brings Warren Beatty back from the dead to quarterback the team. I applaud his decision.

Fast-forward to 1980.

My Rams have made it all the way. Like all Super Bowls, this one is maddeningly scheduled on Sunday evening. Torn, I make the devout choice and go to church services. But the last amen is my signal for a fly pattern to the car radio, which tells me even early in the third quarter that the Pittsburgh Steelers are holding all the aces. Los Angeles is just a sacrificial ram.

Fast-forward to 1999.

The Rams have gotten out of sinful Southern California, landing in a city with "Saint" in its name. After all those glamour boys at quarterback – even a touch of Joe Namath – they've picked up a nobody from a nothing league.

Turns out he's a Christian, and not afraid to say so.

He's not afraid to throw the ball, either, and the Rams finally win a real Super Bowl.

So now everybody's a Rams fan. And Kurt Warner is an example of Christian success.

What I want to know is, will this ruin my team? You know how trends go in sports. If the Rams win with a Christian image, will the rest of the NFL start hunting their own players of faith?

Or if they don't, will Christians start flocking to the Rams by the thousands? Is it possible that in a year or two most of the Rams' fans will not really know or care much about pro football, but that they'll only profess to be fans because it's the socially acceptable thing to do?

Will this lead to home games where most of the seats go to people who aren't excited about being in the stadium, and who start looking at their watches in the third quarter?

Even with a guy like Kurt Warner, you see how this could drag down the team.

A true fan, like me, will only have two choices. One, try to drive away those who don't look sincere, those I think are just filling seats on Sunday.

Two, find some way to light their hearts with the same fire I've had for the Rams since I was a kid.

Tough call. I wonder if churches have a page in their playbooks for this situation.

"Consider the ravens: They do not sow or reap, they have no storeroom or barn; yet God feeds them." Luke 12:24

08.31.2002: Without naming names, the Bible says plenty to fans of pro football

The National Football League begins its regular season next week. Its fans need help. Well, that kind, too, but I meant they need help finding new excuses to feed their spouses.

So here's a new tactic: "But, honey, I have to watch the game to increase my Bible knowledge. After all, it's Sunday." Maybe she'll buy that, given this supporting evidence.

Below are the number of biblical references to each NFL team. I consulted both New International and King James versions, and listed the greater of the two.

Chiefs, 336. Not an Indian among them, but lots of priests and army captains.

Rams, 167. They usually end up dead and burned.

Saints, 98. Romans mentions "Saints, given to hospitality." Which describes New Orleans' usual play.

Lions, 84. David was called Lion of Judah. Today he'd have been an NFL quarterback.

Eagles, 34. Fast, fierce and enduring. But not kosher.

Chargers, 19. Archaic word in the KJV means a fancy bowl or platter, like the one John the Baptist's head was served on.

Giants, 19. Mostly lived in Gath, home of Goliath, a famous middle linebacker.

Colts, 17. The one Jesus rode into Jerusalem got more cheers than Indianapolis typically gets in a season, even with young hosses like Edgerrin James.

Bears, 16. Usually mean, sometimes deadly.

Ravens, 12. Proverbs warns one will peck out your eyes if you sass your parents. Good football imagery.

Raiders, 7. They attacked out of Moab every year.

Redskins, 6. Surprised? Part of the Israelites' tabernacle was ram skins dyed red. (They'll have to kill the Rams first.)

Steelers, 4. Well, four references to steel. Two mention a steel bow broken by strong hands – a portent of bad things for Kordell Stewart's passing?

Falcons, 3.

Browns, 3. Mostly animals. Jacob, for example, got to sort his father-in-law's herds and keep the spotted ones and the speckleds and the browns.

Jaguars, 0. If a leopard is close enough, count eight. Fast and mean, except when they lie down with the goats – about midway through the playoffs.

Texans, 0. If the Houston expansion team had taken the traditional franchise name, it could have racked up 203 references to oil and moved ahead of the Rams on this list. Having lived in that state, I imagine many Texans are shocked to learn that the Bible does not mention them.

Titans, 0. If this team had kept the name it had …

Cowboys, 0. Another Texas team the Bible pointedly does not mention.

Other zeroes: Patriots (change to New England Zealots, get four references), Dolphins (nor porpoises), Bills (nor buffalo), Jets (but four biblical names begin with Jet), Bengals (nor generic tigers), Broncos (but plenty of horses), Cardinals (nor red birds), Seahawks (but three hawks), 49ers, Packers, Vikings, Panthers, Buccaneers.

During halftime and beer commercials, pull out your Bible and check my scoring. Maybe you'll learn something.

" 'For I know the plans I have for you,' declares the LORD,
'plans to prosper you and not to harm you, plans to give you
hope and a future.' " Jeremiah 29:11

01.03.2004: Take a lesson in chess from a player who just lost once

Only once in four years did I compete for the glory of my high school. I did not run, swim, wrestle or play football, baseball or basketball. I did not even debate or judge livestock.

But one day the top-ranked player on my high school chess team got sick just before a big match.

This meant that our No. 2 player would have to move up and take on the other team's No. 1, our No. 3 against their No. 2 and so on. This meant we would get clobbered.

The chess coach decided a better strategy was to use me as his secret weapon. He asked me to join the team just for this one match and take over that No. 1 spot as sort of a sacrificial lamb. He figured I'd get squashed, but at least the real team members wouldn't have to play over their heads – and maybe they could pull out a team victory.

Coach Yoder had never seen me play chess, though. Against terrific odds I played my heart out. I should have played my brains out instead, because after 15 minutes my king was down for the count.

I was never asked to play competitive chess again. My lifetime record stands at 0-1.

I am determined, however, not to let that stop me from sharing a lesson from the game of chess. The lesson is that famed players such as Fischer, Kasparov and Karpov – members of the elite handful ranked as grandmasters by the World Chess Federation – share an ability to look at the chess board and see farther into the future than you or I can.

This is why I can beat my 9-year-old son, who looks only one move into the future.

This is why you can beat me if you look three moves into the future.

This is why Kasparov, looking four or five moves into the future, can demolish the rest of humanity.

And this is why a computer, programmed to select the most advantageous move after looking five or six steps into the future, can frustrate Kasparov.

He who looks farthest into the future – and is able to act wisely now on what he perceives will happen there – becomes the most powerful force in the game.

So how powerful a force are you in day-to-day life, a game much more complicated than pushing pawns and rooks around 64 little squares?

When you're trying to make the wisest decision, trying to consider what the consequences of your words and actions are going to be, how many moves into the future are you able to see? Two, three, four?

In chess you can nurture this ability and get better with each passing game.

Life, however, you play only once. The learning curve is dreadfully steep. Which is why you might want to consider using your secret weapon.

God is able to look from one end of eternity to the other and evaluate simultaneously the consequences and ramifications of every move you make. He's an omniscient grandmaster, and he's taking applications for anyone interested in being on his team.

I may be a loser, but that looks like a good move to me.

"Jesus said to his disciples: 'Things that cause people to sin are
bound to come, but woe to that person through whom they
come. It would be better for him to be thrown into the sea with
a millstone tied around his neck than for him to cause one of
these little ones to sin. So watch yourselves.' " Luke 17:1-3

03.09.2002: Baseball season's here, when kids' coaches pray for winning attitudes

These are the times that try men's souls.

It's time to start kid baseball and softball again. I just got the list of 7- and 8-year-olds I'll be managing this spring. A promising season for the Minor B Yankees.

Of course, every March looks promising. Maybe that's why these times try men's souls so deeply.

The men I'm talking about are mostly good guys. They volunteer their time to coach thousands of boys and girls. I'm part of this crowd. In fact, there's not much to make me stand out in this crowd. Not skills. Not the ability to motivate. Not my win-loss record. Not my attitude.

It's attitude that troubles me at this time of year. I'm getting psyched up. I want to do a good job. I want to set a good example. I want to teach the boys some skills. I want to win some games.

There's nothing wrong with those components of my attitude, even the part about winning. But in early March it's an untested attitude. It's fresh off the shelf, as stiff and clean as a pair of baseball pants before the first practice in the red clay.

But what I know, somewhere in the back of my mind, is that as the season runs its course I will get sucked in.

The part about wanting to teach the boys some skills will come face to face with the fact that a couple of the boys just want to be left alone to dig for bugs in the outfield, and that a line drive rolling to their feet is an unwelcome distraction. The third or tenth time that happens, my attitude will crumple a bit, pick up a few stains.

And the part about wanting to win some games will become sharper as the weeks roll by. Without extreme care it will become so sharp that it will put holes in both knees of my attitude. I'll holler something I shouldn't. I'll question a call I should let slide. I'll start a quiet feud with another coach who in March was as well-intentioned as I was.

In a way, kid baseball offers a microcosm for my spiritual role in the world at large. Which suggests these points worth considering:

Quitting is not the solution. Few enough good men are involved in the lives of children as it is. Grow, don't quit.

When Jesus sent workers out, he did it in pairs. Seek out other coaches who share your values. Draw strength from each other.

Declare yourself publicly. Tell those little players and their parents early what standards you want to be held to.

Pray. For the kids. For the parents. For yourself.

Sending a bunch of testosterone-crazed men out to the diamond to teach impressionable children about sports may be less prudent than having a Weight Watchers meeting on buffet night at the Pizza Hut. (That amen you hear is from our spouses.) But, as in the rest of our lives, we're the only tools God has to get this job done.

So, all you coaches with a conscience, get out there and give it your best shot. Play hurt if you have to. Focus on the fundamentals of your faith.

Keep your eye on the ball.

"For I have the desire to do what is good, but I cannot carry it out. For what I do is not the good I want to do; no, the evil I do not want to do – this I keep on doing." Romans 7:18-19

07.06.2002: Another season come and gone, and still I can barely manage

In March, with a new baseball season full of promise, I wrote about the 7- and 8-year-old Yankees I was about to manage. About how hard it is to coach and keep a Christian attitude. I promised to give it my best shot.

With the season over, I feel obligated to tell you how it went.

Only one statistic really matters in coaching, of course – and my Yankees went 8-8. Some of those were nailbiters, and we could just as easily been 12-4. Or 4-12.

Still, it was a great season.

We turned a legitimate double play. Turned a triple play, too.

Watched a kid who'd never played before blast out a triple late in the year. He got thrown out trying to come home, and cried in the dugout for 15 minutes, not believing that the runs he drove in won the game.

We hit our stride and won three in a row by the 10-run rule and looked like we should be playing on TV.

We lost our focus and lost three in a row and looked like we should just go home and watch cartoons.

We kept the pressure off, like the day we played Whiffle-ball with mothers and grandmas and siblings.

Later, when the pressure was on, and the baseball had to be thrown to exactly the right spot, my guys came through, repeatedly knocking me into the dunking booth.

But it wasn't all fun and games. In trying to model a spiritual attitude, I'm not sure I did much better than 8-8.

I didn't actually yell at the umpire, but I glared a lot, and when I couldn't believe the call I let out a loud "Oh!" We won't even talk about my thoughts.

Playing night games when my players should have been in bed, I demanded focus as if they were capable of giving it.

The Yankees did not win the league Sportsmanship Trophy, nor did I hear a single "Oh!" in protest of our non-selection. We were a little too rowdy, our coaches a little too intense.

And just as most casual watchers couldn't tell what good sports we Yankees really were, my Christianity went mostly unnoticed, too.

It showed up sometimes, in little ways, as when the umpire didn't show up and the coaches took turns behind home plate. Not a single argument arose all night, and I was proud of both teams.

Still, as I wrote back in March, sending a bunch of testosterone-crazed men out to teach children about sports is like reading Edgar Allen Poe stories to help the tykes go to sleep. Scary.

So to all of you coaches who just finished a tough season, and who weren't the constant, glowing Christian example you told yourself you'd be in the preseason, I just want to say, don't give up.

Paul knew the struggle, too, and said, "For what I do is not the good I want to do; no, the evil I do not want to do – this I keep on doing." And Paul felt that way even without getting hit on a shin by some kid swinging a bat in the dugout.

So don't be too hard on yourselves; God needs somebody to work with these kids.

It's almost soccer season.

SECTION SEVEN:
CHILDISHNESS

"At that time Jesus, full of joy through the Holy Spirit, said, 'I praise you, Father, Lord of heaven and earth, because you have hidden these things from the wise and learned, and revealed them to little children. Yes, Father, for this was your good pleasure.' " Luke 10:21

10.12.2002: Excuse me for acting childishly, but it's something I've got to do

I like children because they sing even if they do not know the words.

Because if something is hanging out of your nose they will tell you. They will laugh, but they will tell you.

Because they lift their arms to the sky, begging to be picked up and held.

Because they will raptly listen to any story that falls under the heading of "Something That Happened to You When You Were Little, Daddy."

Because the only thing they hate more than getting into a bathtub is getting out of a bathtub.

Because if you take them to the Grand Canyon they will not be so fascinated by the ribbon of water far below that they overlook the just-as-fascinating ribbon of ants heading for a dropped potato chip.

Because not only do they not care whether they are dirty or sticky, they do not even know. Truly.

Because they believe in Band-Aids.

Because they know how to express their feelings. Even tantrums serve a purpose, after all.

Because they know how to switch their feelings. Even a tantrum can metamorphose into a giggle in 3.8 seconds.

Because they are curious about God. And heaven. And angels. And the details of Daniel's night with those lions. And the details of Adam and Eve's days in the Garden.

I like children because, even if you agree with the concept of Original Sin, there is something about them that suggests a kiss of Eden.

Wasn't it childlike things that made it paradise? That you could be dirty or sticky and not know it? That God would take you for a walk every day and tell you stories about things he'd seen and done?

Jesus indisputably had a special appreciation for wee ones. "Whoever welcomes one of these little children in my name welcomes me," he said.

Trying to get through to his enemies, Jesus once reminded them that even they knew how to give good gifts to their children.

I don't understand everything that Jesus had in mind when he fussed at his oh-so-adult followers one busy day: "Let the little children come to me, and do not hinder them, for the kingdom of heaven belongs to such as these."

I know there are elements of innocence and blind trust, and maybe that's all Jesus meant. But maybe its more layered than that: the way a child lives for the moment, the excitement about life, the lack of self-consciousness.

Maybe there are more layers that I can't see, try as I might, simply because I am an adult. Jesus once praised his father because "you have hidden these things from the wise and learned, and revealed them to little children."

Children responded to Jesus, too. When he arrived in Jerusalem for the last time in his life, it was the children in the temple area shouting "Hosanna!" that set his oh-so-adult enemies to grumbling.

I wonder if I could still pull that off today – acting like a hosanna-filled child in this world of grumbling adults.

"One of them, when he saw he was healed, came back, praising God in a loud voice. He threw himself at Jesus' feet and thanked him – and he was a Samaritan. Jesus asked, 'Were not all ten cleansed? Where are the other nine? Was no one found to return and give praise to God except this foreigner?' " Luke 17:15-18

12.23.2000: Teach those little package-rippers how to say thanks for gifts received

The signs are easy to spot.

Children rip through presents like a tornado, barely slowing down enough to read a label before grabbing another box from beneath the tree.

They are brutally honest: "No, this isn't the one I wanted. The one with karate-chop action is cool; this one's dopey."

They do not say thank you on Christmas morning or in the quieter aftermath.

Not with murmured words and not with a hasty e-mail and certainly not with a formal letter or card.

These are the unmistakable signs that, yes, these are our children.

And we cannot blame them, not in their early years, for their rudeness. We adults know we have helped push our children into an addiction to receiving.

Being blessed is a habit for them, and they have so much that they really don't understand the concept of saying thank you.

But don't despair! These greedy little blobs can grow into appreciative adults if we model the correct attitudes. Christmas is as good a time to start as any. Let the little tykes know that you know how to offer a proper thank you for gifts received ...

Dear God,

We had a great Christmas here in Alabama. I hope you had a great Christmas in Heaven. We had a little snow this week, so it really felt like Christmas.

Does it snow in Heaven?

I am writing to thank you for the gifts you sent me. You really shouldn't have, but they were all great and I really like them.

Thank you for the Earth. It's neat because I can use it for so many different things. Sometimes I just like to look at it. It makes me think of you. Sorry about the parts that got messed up, but I think they can be fixed.

Thank you for the family. I have to admit it wasn't the one I marked in the catalog, but the more I play with it the more I like it. None of my friends has one I'd trade for, that's for sure. And thank you for the accessories, too, like the house and the cars and the kitchen full of food. I'll bet it's sort of like your house. Please send me a picture so I can compare.

Thank you for the book. I haven't been reading as much as I should, but I'll bet it has a happy ending. My favorite character so far is David, but I'm only about halfway through. Do you think they'll make a movie out if it?

Thank you for the comforter. It's given me a lot of warmth.

Thank you for the savior. You know how sometimes you don't even know that you need something, but once you get it you wonder how you ever got along without it? That's the way it is with the savior. Oh, and thank you for the grace that came with the savior. They're a perfect match.

Well, guess I'd better run. Sorry I didn't get you anything, especially after all of the gifts you had for me. Is there anything you want? You name it and I'll do my best to give it to you.

Thanks again, and I hope I can come see you real soon.

"My heart is in anguish within me; the terrors of death assail me. Fear and trembling have beset me; horror has overwhelmed me. I said, 'Oh, that I had the wings of a dove! I would fly away and be at rest.' " Psalm 55:4-6

03.24.2001: What do you say to a child who has just learned that goldfish die?

Moses the goldfish has died.

He lived a short life – less than a year – and probably a lonely life. But he had all the fish flakes he could eat and a scenic view of the kitchen through his glass bowl. You see and hear some interesting stuff in a family kitchen.

Dime-store goldfish don't expect much more out of life, so I did not cry at Moses' funeral, a brief affair in the front bathroom. I was the only mourner, and I didn't know what to say, so I just sent him on his way amid the sounds of rushing water.

Then I rinsed out his bowl for the next inhabitant.

Cade, who is 3 1/2, named Moses. He did not say where the name came from, but between the stories of the bulrushes and the Red Sea, I suspect that Moses is simply the Sunday school character he most associates with water.

Moses had been on death watch for a few days, since my wife, Janet, noticed he was swimming sort of sideways. When she told Cade that Moses had gotten sick and died, Cade said he wanted to see him.

He didn't say anything at his first glimpse of death, but after Janet left the room for a minute, she returned to find Cade lying atop his sad-eyed, long-suffering dog, hugging her tightly.

Later that morning, he asked the obvious, dreaded question, "Mommy, am I going to get sick?"

What is the right answer?

No, you are going to live forever and ever. And you'll always be with Mommy and Daddy, and we'll always be a happy family, and we'll never let anybody hurt you, and we'll keep away any yucky stuff that could make you sick.

Even the Children's Television Workshop has deeper theology.

Yes, you are going to get sick, and then you are going to die. But don't worry, people live a lot longer than fishes.

That's not exactly true, since no matter how many years you spend, when the end approaches most people look back and say it passed by in a flash. Fish years, dog years, people years, they're all short in the end.

No, God wouldn't let a sweet little boy like you get sick and die like Moses.

That's not true, either, is it? You can't return to any 10-year college reunion and expect 100 percent participation. You can't return to many 10-year high school reunions and expect everybody to be there. And sadly enough, death will already have disrupted many 10-year preschool reunions, if anybody plans such events.

Yes, you are going to die someday. That's why it's important to love other people and try to do the right things, so that God will give you a new place to live.

That's true, but how do you tell a little boy that when most adults can't get it through their skins deeply enough to change their lives?

No, son, I hope not.

That's the answer on many a parent's lips, even as stomachs sink and prayers rise.

Meanwhile, Cade says that no, he does not want to buy another Moses.

Why not, Cade? "Because another one's going to die."

*"Are not five sparrows sold for two pennies? Yet not one of
them is forgotten by God. Indeed, the very hairs of your head
are all numbered. Don't be afraid; you are worth more than
many sparrows." Luke 12:6-7*

11.16.2002: This 5-year-old will face issues
more tangled than curly hair

He is 5 now, and works it into most sentences. "I can do it by
myself. I'm 5, you know."

Or conversely, "I don't have to do that anymore. I'm 5."

Or simply, to a passing stranger, "Hi, I'm 5."

The ease with which he talks to just about anyone, of any
age, about anything embarrasses his older brothers. They are
more likely to duck their heads when an adult speaks to them.

Cade doesn't have time for such hang-ups. After all, 5-year-
olds lead busy lives. Besides, he is a beautiful child who knows
that his smile and eyes can win him a place in any heart.
Everybody loves Cade.

He has great skin, a broad, easy smile and the longest real
eyelashes I've ever seen on a human being.

A few months ago, I'd have described his soft, curly hair, too.
His curls contributed to his beauty, as acquaintances and
strangers alike often told him.

But Cade did not share that opinion of his curls. He knew that
they made him different, that his mother and his father and his
brothers all had straight hair. Cade wanted straight hair, too.

Like most 5-year-olds, Cade finds many uses for the
bathroom sink: mud-pie mixing bowl, action-figure swimming
pool, marble-washing station. But sometimes over the past year,
if he disappeared into the bathroom and closed the door, it was to
wet his curls and plaster them against his forehead. "Look, I have
straight hair, too," he'd say. And for a few minutes he was happy
with his hair.

But Cade knew that a longer-lasting solution was needed
(After all, he's 5, you know). Finally, a few months ago, on a visit

to the salon, he convinced his mother to let the lady cut off his curls.

"Look," he told me when I got home that day, "Straight hair!"

True enough. Stubble short, but straight. Just like the rest of the family.

You'll probably never meet Cade, and you've certainly lost your chance to see his curls, but you and I both know that the amount of wave in your hair has absolutely nothing to do with your worth as a person, your beauty in the sight of God or man, or your acceptance into a family or a society. It's just hair, and it has good days and bad days no matter what texture or length it is.

But Cade won't buy that line. Even though a pair of clippers has solved the problem for him, it still makes me sad when I think about his hair.

Not because of the curls, really, but because I'm afraid that at some age after 5 he'll start being bothered by other differences between himself and the rest of his family.

He can talk about what it means that he's adopted, but he doesn't know that there's anything especially significant about the fact that he is biracial – half Caucasian, half African-American.

I plan to tell him that race, like hair, has nothing to do with his worth or beauty.

But I'm afraid he won't buy that unless an awful lot of people are willing to back me up.

"And in their prayers for you their hearts will go out to you,
because of the surpassing grace God has given you."
2 Corinthians 9:14

01.11.2003: One more little example of how
God's grace uses the littlest things

A new baby just arrived at my house. She is a little thing, but
I have big hopes that somehow, some day, she will play a big role
in God's plan. God, after all, being full of grace, has a history of
using little things to accomplish a lot.

A few little examples you might remember from Sunday
school:

A little boy with a little sling and a little stone became a
giant-killer.

A little bit of oil became a widow's overflowing blessing in
Elisha's hands.

Another little bit of oil, plus a little flour, became a widow's
overflowing pantry in Elijah's hands.

A little dust became a man, a little bone became a woman. A
little fruit became a big problem.

A pair of little coins helped Jesus teach a great lesson about
generosity.

A little bone from a donkey became a weapon of mass
destruction when Samson fought on Jawbone Hill.

A little vine showed Jonah a lesson that was too big for the
whale to teach.

A muddy little river taught the leprous Naaman about the
great God from whom all blessings clearly flow.

A little faith was enough to get Peter walking on water.

A little mustard seed stands as the most famous example of
what a little faith, like Peter's, can grow into.

A little cloud the size of a fist became a great rainstorm,
helping Elijah prove that evil King Ahab was all wet.

Later, a little whisper finished the job of proving to Elijah that God was omnipotent. Not a mighty wind, not an earthquake, not a roaring fire; just a gentle little whisper.

A little lamb was worth leaving a whole flock behind and mounting a search for it.

A little fish and bread became a great buffet. Thousands served.

A little baby laid in a little manger in a little stable in a little village in a little province in a great empire became the ruler of an infinitely greater empire.

Little by little, these examples ought to add up. They ought to convince me that a gracious God places the greatest emphasis on the littlest things.

They ought to convince me, but I still keep trying to be a big man, an important man. I'm afraid the Bible's many little examples do not soak in, even when Paul looks over the church and reminds its members to "think of what you were when you were called. Not many of you were wise by human standards; not many were influential; not many were of noble birth." In other words, just a bunch of little people – who put themselves in big hands.

Or, as Jesus once asserted, pointing to a little boy, "Unless you change and become like little children, you will never enter the kingdom of heaven.

Therefore, whoever humbles himself like this child is the greatest."

There is a big lesson in that, and I have a little baby at my house to teach it to me again.

Her first name, by the way, is Hailey.

But her middle name is Grace.

"Let your gentleness be evident to all. The Lord is near. Do not be anxious about anything, but in everything, by prayer and petition, with thanksgiving, present your requests to God."
                                        Philippians 4:5-6

04.03.2004: I'm a little fuzzy on how to pray for the bunny

"Say a prayer for the Easter Bunny, Dad."

That's the latest from the 6-year-old at my house. I'm inclined to honor his request, especially because he's having a rough spring.

His tadpole died.

His favorite dog jumped the fence one too many times and had to go live elsewhere.

He broke the rules in kindergarten one too many times and had to bring home a note from his teacher, so his mother made him write an apology. Instead, he wrote, "Mess T this is my laste da to kum to sool I ame gowing to go to a nooe sool." His spelling gets worse under duress, but that translates to, "Ms. T, this is my last day to come to school. I am going to go to a new school. Love, Cade."

Later he was given a second disciplinary note to bring home, but he hid that one in the classroom trash can. When my wife and Ms. T found it, across the bottom he'd scrawled in desperation, "I did nothing."

Yes, life is rough on kids – even if they have both parents at home, nobody is beating them, there's plenty of food and clean underwear, they know how to pray and their teachers are kind.

So I'm glad kids have diversions like Santa, the Tooth Fairy and the Easter Bunny to brighten their days. I imagine that trio does less harm than believing in pro wrestling, "Joe Millionaire" and miracle diets.

But what kind of a prayer am I supposed to offer on behalf of the Easter Bunny? Here are my options.

1. Steer the myth into Christianity, like this: "Oh Lord who created all creatures from the mighty elephant to the tiny rabbit,

and who is the true giver of all that is sweet and good, we thank you for the Easter Bunny, a symbol of the overflowing joy we feel during this season of renewal, when life is resurrected all around us as a reminder of your precious son."

2. Explain the truth. But he's only 6, and if I pull the plug on the Easter Bunny, will his simple mind decide that Jonah and Lazarus and Goliath are also just silly stories I've made up?

3. Pray to the bunny instead, like this: "Oh, dear Easter Bunny, we've tried to be good, so we ask you to bring us lots of treats next week. But please, Easter Bunny, don't let the dog get into the chocolate this year." That seems sacrilegious even by my loose standards.

4. Change the subject, like this: "Well, right now I think we should pray instead for the millions of souls in China who haven't heard the good news. And for the hungry children in Africa." That would certainly begin to engrain in his mind the idea many adults still have, that God cares only about the big picture and not about what's really on their minds.

5. Honor the request at face value, like this: "Oh Lord, Cade asks that you bless the Easter Bunny. Amen." That seems like the best option, so long as it is followed by another, silent prayer, like this:

"Oh Lord, this little boy believes in you. Please give me wisdom to keep that faith growing as he grows. Even if the other tadpole dies. Amen."

"The length of our days is seventy years – or eighty, if we have the strength; yet their span is but trouble and sorrow, for they quickly pass, and we fly away." Psalm 90:10

08.05.2000: When you reach the top of life's roller coaster, ask for directions

Forget about how astute you are not, how self-aware you are not.

Eventually, you and just about everyone else will reach that point when the roller coaster of life teeters for a moment at the top. Your eyes open wider and you realize with a wrench in your gut that the ride is half over.

From way up here you can see for miles, or years, in both directions. Where you've been, where you're going.

Then the car lurches forward, tilts down, and with each passing millisecond you revise your estimate of just how short the rest of the ride will be.

Men like to call this defining moment "a midlife crisis," but it's little more than the metaphoric equivalent of screaming at the top of your lungs and jerking in your seat with terror before the roller coaster plummets. No matter how much you squirm and clutch, you aren't getting out of that seat, and the ride operator isn't going to stop and let you off.

To reach this teetering moment at the top, which ironically so many people see as a deep valley in their lives, you generally need to be as far from the start of life as you assume you are from the end.

If you're an average guy who thinks you'll live to be 80 or 90, divide that time by 2 and expect it to hit you in your 40s.

But even if you're the ultimate optimist, well before you hit 65 you'll be old enough to understand that you are indeed going to die. Not only that, but you are going to die in less time than it has taken you to get to this point in your life.

This realization sinks in because now you've ridden far enough to look down the track and see the end of the ride.

Knowing you only have 45 years left takes on concrete meaning when you've already lived 45 years and can play back in your mind how swiftly it zipped past.

Now a decision is waiting to be made. It will still be there waiting if you need to take a few weeks or months first to test-drive the Corvette, or enlist in the Hair Club for Men, or learn to line dance, or whatever other screaming and jerking your particular midlife crisis entails.

The decision is, where are you going?

It's not an easy decision to make as you gather momentum and life zips you ever faster down the hill.

But luckily, in life as opposed to amusement park rides, it is a decision you get to make.

In life you can steer. You can't make a U-turn and go back the way you came, but you can steer. And there are a lot of roads to pick.

So if you feel that midlife crisis coming on, maybe it's because you aren't sure what your destination is, or how you're going to get there.

You could probably head off the crisis by doing something simple. Ask God to point you in the way you should go.

Too simple?

Oh, well, we all know how stubborn men are about asking for directions.

"Let him live with the animals among the plants of the earth. Let his mind be changed from that of a man and let him be given the mind of an animal." Daniel 4:15-16

07.20.2002: You've got higher lessons to learn than these from animal kingdom

Time now for lessons from the animal kingdom. I'll stay here while you go on ahead ...

Armadillos can retreat into impenetrable armor, where they are safe from predators. But they can't get any work done that way. Don't be like an armadillo.

Llamas can spit for distance and accuracy. This is a satisfying way to mark your enemies. But once the spit lleaves your llips, you can't call it back. Don't be like a llama.

Planaria are tiny worms that can grow two heads if a split develops in the one they start life with. This lets them see problems from more than one perspective. But it makes it twice as hard to decide which direction to swim. Don't be like a planarium.

Octopi can squirt a cloud of dark liquid. This gives them something to hide behind. But it also makes it difficult to give an octopus a hug. Don't be like an octopus.

Dogs stay cool by panting. They're only comfortable if their tongues are flapping. Don't be like a dog.

Moths can unfailingly navigate by using the brightest light of the night sky. But they don't have the depth perception to tell the difference between the moon 238,000 miles away and a 75-watt bulb over the garage door. Don't be like a moth.

Manatees are curious, and often pop up beside motorboats to see what's happening. This makes manatees popular among tourists and other "happening" people. But many manatees become deeply scarred before learning that curiosity and propellers don't mix. Don't be like a manatee.

Beavers have four sharp teeth that never stop growing. This makes a beaver into nature's chainsaw. But if a beaver ever ceases his endless chewing and gnawing, his incisors will outgrow his head. Don't be like a beaver.

Mike the parakeet lives in a cage next to my television set. This means he is exposed to all kinds of interesting dialogue. But when Mike talks, it sounds like nothing but the background babble of a crowded room, with no distinct words, no meaning. Don't be like Mike.

Some lizards have a tail that breaks off easily. This makes the lizard tougher for an enemy to grab. But how wise is it to fall to pieces whenever someone surprises you? Don't be like a lizard.

Cows have complicated digestive systems. They can hold onto something that's already been chewed and bring it up again and again. Don't be like a cow.

Some birds, like the cuckoo, lay their eggs among another bird's eggs. The little cuckoos are then cared for by a sort of foster mother, leaving the adult cuckoos free for other pursuits. True, baby birds are noisy, messy and ugly. Still, don't be like a cuckoo.

A falling cat, will almost always twist to land on its feet. This keeps cats from getting dirty. But this also lets cats exude an arrogance that keeps people from offering help when it's needed. Don't be like a cat.

A thought: Instead of imitating animals, be like the one in whose image you're animated.

SECTION EIGHT:
CHURCH POTLUCK

"So whether you eat or drink or whatever you do, do it all for the glory of God." 1 Corinthians 10:31

07.10.2004: You can tell the health of a church by its potlucks

Judging the spiritual health of a church is more of an art than a science.

Some of the leading indicators can be deceiving.

I've known churches with bank statements that were balanced only in the sense that a house of cards is balanced, yet some of them had a fire in the belly to sustain them through the leanest of times.

I've known churches with beautiful campuses that made them the picture of health, until you realized that the beauty was easy to maintain because so few people ever walked on the perfect grass or entered the pristine buildings.

That's why I prefer a more accurate indicator: the church potluck. Fellowship meal, dinner on the grounds, covered-dish supper – call it what you like, just don't call me late for it. As the Good Book suggests, I'm like a roaring lion, seeking what I may devour.

Participation is the first half of this indicator. At healthy churches, most everyone stays to eat, even if it's not easy to do so. That holds true even if the dining area is too small or the sun is too hot or there's a big game on TV.

If a big chunk of the membership turns its back on the shared luncheon, heading instead to some predictable restaurant for a private meal, that's a danger sign.

On the other hand, if people stay to eat even if they came to church with no casserole or Crock Pot or cake to contribute, that's a sign of health. At solid churches, if you try to duck out because you forgot to cook, someone is sure to say, "Come on ahead. I brought plenty for both of us."

The second half of this indicator is whether that friend who says she brought plenty is telling the truth.

If you dawdle along and end up in the back of the line, last to get your paper plate, you'll be in a perfect position to judge this factor. It's a given that Sister Smith's melt-in-your-mouth sweet potatoes will be long gone by then, but if there's still plenty of tempting food, that's a healthy church. A church that needs an exercise ministry, perhaps, but a healthy church nonetheless.

On the other hand, if the last few people in line have to fill up on lima beans and Hawaiian Spam Delight, there might be a problem. Long ago when I was a newlywed, I went to a Sunday school potluck with a load of other newlywed couples. It was the only time I've ever seen the food completely run out before everyone had been served. The reason is obvious – we were all too inexperienced and self-absorbed to know better.

Experiences like that make me worry about the long-term prospects for the church potluck. Some congregations now hire caterers. Some direct families just to bring their own fast food and forget about sharing. Even at traditional fellowship meals, more KFC buckets are showing up and fewer of the pies are homemade.

Sometimes I get so worried about the vanishing sacrament of potluck that I can barely eat.

Unless that's coconut cream pie up ahead.

"Speaking the truth in love, we will in all things grow up into him who is the Head, that is, Christ. From him the whole body, joined and held together by every supporting ligament, grows and builds itself up in love, as each part does its work."
Ephesians 4:15-16

09.24.2004: A theory of evolution that helps churches grow

What we need in our local churches is more evolution of the species.

This kind of gradual change is already at work, but if a

church wants to survive, grow and blossom it needs to find ways to encourage more evolution, maybe even speed it up.

Field research shows us these four common species:

1. Be quiet and patient, and out on the fringes you'll catch glimpses of the rabbits. Don't wait until after the final amen of the Sunday morning service, because they'll be gone before you open your eyes and turn your head.

They hop in and out, keeping to the back pews, wary of the open space where somebody might ask them for a commitment.

They know something is missing in their lives, but they aren't certain what. So they nervously nibble a bit here, then try a bit over there, looking for the perfect spiritual food. Leave a bad taste in their mouths – "The sermon was too dry," "Those people aren't friendly," "I don't fit in" – and they'll bolt out the back door for good.

2. Many of the rabbits who do not bolt eventually evolve into sheep. Feeling secure and comfortable now inside the church building, they graze contentedly. They have their favorite pews, which they faithfully visit week after week, and a small sub-herd of other sheep they seek out who make them feel they are part of something personal and familial.

No longer do they hide in the back pews or flee at the approach of a stranger, but they are still primarily concerned with being fed – and if they get hungry enough they'll run off in a group to some greener pasture.

3. Fortunately, some of these sheep, the ones who don't have a baaad experience, evolve into sheep dogs. They take responsibility for keeping the sheep from wandering off. Some churches give them the title of deacons, ministry leaders, lay leaders, committee chairs. Evolution has given them a higher metabolism than the sheep, and they stay on the run most of the time, chasing from one crisis to the next, trying to sustain order and happiness in their little sector of the congregation.

4. The sheep dogs that don't run themselves to death sometimes evolve into shepherds. The New Testament also calls them pastors, elders, presbyters and a few other honorable titles.

Their legs may not be as strong as those courageous sheep dogs, but they make up for it with an extra dose of wisdom, knowing from experience which crises need attention and which will take care of themselves. The gentlest can stroke a rabbit without it jumping away.

You can buy a lot of books to describe this sort of inter-species evolution in greater detail, and if it makes you feel better you can send me the cash you would have spent.

In a nutshell, though, a growing church must find ways to turn its rabbits into sheep before they hop away. Those sheep must be stroked and encouraged until they become sheep dogs. Those sheep dogs must be prayed for and appreciated until they become shepherds.

It's the kind of evolution the Good Shepherd would approve of.

"Him who overcomes I will make a pillar in the temple of my God. Never again will he leave it." Revelation 3:12

05:26.2001: It's hard to resist putting St. Simeon on a pedestal, but we ought to try

Putting historical Christian figures on a pedestal is not a wise practice, but for Simeon Stylites you sort of have to make an exception.

Actually, three saints bore that name.

The first was a shepherd boy born in Syria around 388. He entered a monastery at 16, but went so far overboard in his austerity that the other monks kicked him out.

And so St. Simeon the Elder became the first of the "pillar hermits" who raised holiness to new heights.

He started out by restricting himself to living in a desert spot 20 yards in diameter. No leaving under any circumstances. But too many pilgrims showed up, pestering him.

He solved the problem by having a pillar built with a tiny platform on top.

This first pillar (or *stylos* in Greek) was 9 feet tall, but Simeon the Elder worked his way up to a 50-footer. There he lived for 36 years without descending.

No roof or other shelter.

No running water.

No cable TV.

You could visit him by climbing a ladder, or you could stand below with other admirers and listen to Simeon preach. During Lent, Simeon gave up all food and drink and remained upright.

And so he tried to draw closer to God.

As did Simeon Stylites the Younger. You shouldn't even have to ask, but no, this was not the son of Simeon the Elder. No relation.

Simeon the Younger went up in the sixth century as a teen-ager and lived aloft for 68 years.

This was a flashy way to give yourself to God. You eliminated every distraction possible from your lifestyle. You sat on your perch and prayed, fasted, contemplated, wrote letters and waited for a better life.

You did not become a stylite lightly.

More mundane believers looked at you with awe and declared you a saint. You motivated them. "What do you mean you're too tired to go to church services today? If Simeon could stand on a pillar for 36 years, you can drag yourself out of bed one day a week!"

Still, the market for stylites was small. After all, if every Christian was in isolation, what would become of the world?

That's probably a question we need to keep asking today.

What becomes of the world if Christians do more sitting in church buildings than walking on unholy ground?

What becomes of the world if the Bible Belt becomes a black hole, sucking all of the Christians into a tiny portion of the planet so that they can live amid other believers?

What becomes of the world if all of the Christians leave the public schools, to be educated elsewhere?

What becomes of the world if we all climb pillars?

But I almost forgot. I said there were three men named Simeon Stylites. Not much is known about the third, who lived in the fifth century.

And maybe it doesn't mean anything ominous, but this Simeon was sitting on his pillar when lightning struck him.

"His intent was that now, through the church, the manifold wisdom of God should be made known to the rulers and authorities in the heavenly realms, according to his eternal purpose which he accomplished in Christ Jesus our Lord."
Ephesians 3:10-11

08.24.2002: Even for grownups, there must be a market out there for toy churches

All he wanted for Christmas was a toy church. He was 3, maybe 4. Because he had been a good boy, and because we were young parents, and because he was our first child, and because we wanted to nurture his spiritual side, we tried to give him what he wanted. As we quickly found out, however, Toys 'R Us does not sell toy churches. Nor does KayBee Toys, nor Wal-Mart.

We wanted very much to spoil our son, but that year we had to give up on the toy church.

He got over it, especially since it was just one of those random, momentary visions that dance in little kids' heads, then dance out in less time than it takes for a sugarplum to melt in your mouth.

Forgive me for talking about Christmas while the heat index is over 100 degrees. My wife would vouch that I usually refuse to discuss Christmas gifts until at least Dec. 1. But I remembered that quest for a toy church last week when I pulled into the parking lot of a super-duper home-improvement store. Getting out of the car, I glanced into the bed of the truck parked next to me and saw three wooden churches, each about 2 feet tall at the tip of its little steeple. Each was different, and such an obvious combination of love and skill that I had to wonder what could be missing. What could their creator be buying inside the store to complete these masterpieces?

I never found out. Since my kids are too old to ask for toy churches now, I didn't hang around the parking lot to find out if they were for sale.

It occurs to me that stores may be missing out here. I know I'm not the only person who used to play church as a child, lining up the dining room chairs for pews, maybe finding a few saltines for a communion service. While we waited to be old enough for the real world, we played church, just like we played house and school and circus. This was way before Nintendo, but surely there's a niche market today for toy churches.

It occurs to me also that some of us have grown up and entered the real world, but are still playing church just like we did as kiddies. We like the ceremonies, the rituals and the trappings, but after an hour or so our attention wanes and we're itchy for some other game. Something is missing if we haven't grown from merely playing church to actually being the church, aware at all times and places that we belong to the Creator.

By the way, if we really want to find what's missing from our church life, I'm pretty sure they don't sell it at Lowe's or Home Depot. Building programs with bricks, plywood and nails have their place, but the best way to build up the church is by a home-improvement project on my heart, that home of Christ without which there is no church.

I know I tend to bounce back and forth between a serious commitment to God and shallow, religious play that's more appropriate for a child.

Forgive me, Lord. I guess in more ways than one I'm still looking for that toy church.

"People were bringing little children to Jesus to have him touch them, but the disciples rebuked them. When Jesus saw this, he was indignant. He said to them, 'Let the little children come to me, and do not hinder them, for the kingdom of God belongs to such as these.' " Mark 10:13-14

06.07.2003: May all three of your VBS cookies be homemade

When I was a kid, the ladies of the church stoked their ovens through the warm days of late spring to fill their cookie quotas for vacation Bible school. Life was simpler and calmer back then; boring enough that VBS was a big event in a long, slow summer.

A store-bought cookie at VBS was as rare as Mom saying "Keep it" if she sent us to the store for milk and there was paper money in the change we brought back.

Cookies were an important element of vacation Bible school, almost as important as the metal badges the VBS director awarded each morning to those evangelistic kids who brought visitors.

Like the badges, the cookies were tightly controlled. Each morning before refreshment break, the cookie ladies made a grid of paper napkins on the fellowship hall serving table, then neatly placed three cookies on each napkin.

When we filed through the line we could choose any napkin, but there was no remixing. You scanned for the perfect trio and tried to avoid plain old sugar cookies.

On no other occasion since those vacation Bible schools of my youth have I seen cookies pre-measured like that.

And then it was back to the classrooms, where for five days we glued Popsicle sticks and memorized verses and practiced for the program at which our parents would watch us perform a skit about Lazarus or the prodigal son.

As the last day wound down we'd collect a certificate testifying to successful completion of the curriculum. I found one of those old VBS certificates recently at the bottom of a dusty box of junk, from when I was a fourth-grader in some little cotton town. It's almost as ornate as my high school diploma.

One last time we'd sing, "Booster, booster, be a booster, don't be grouchy like a rooster. Booster, booster, be a booster, and boost our Bible school." It was the loudest we were ever allowed to sing.

Then we'd run out the church doors into the second half of a long, slow summer.

I am amazed that vacation Bible school still exists. The shifting school calendar is shrinking most kids' summer vacations. And even if their summer break is as long as it used to be, it's certainly not as slow. Not with band camps and day camps and sports camps. Not with PlayStation 2 and Instant Messaging.

The world has changed. VBS has changed, too, I guess. Most of the Flannelgraph boards have been replaced by PowerPoint presentations and other hip methods to catch the attention of the kids cramming VBS into their busy summer.

I know times change, and I'm not really a curmudgeon about it. In fact, I hope today they let the kids pick out any cookies they want.

But I hope at last some of those cookies are homemade.

And I hope the kids still sing "Booster, Booster."

And I hope summer is still long and slow enough for them to get bored and appreciate a good week of VBS.

"Sing joyfully to the LORD, you righteous; it is fitting for the upright to praise him. Praise the LORD with the harp; make music to him on the ten-stringed lyre. Sing to him a new song; play skillfully, and shout for joy." Psalm 33:1-3

09.02.2000: Clayton Delaney is probably right about the Lord's taste in music

The great theologian Thomas T. Hall pegged it purty good back in 1971 with these lyrics:

"I remember the year that Clayton Delaney died.
Nobody knew it but I went out in the woods and I cried.
While I know there's a lot of big preachers
that know a lot more than I do,
It could be that the good Lord
likes a little pickin' too."

He was singing about a local musician who had taught him a thing or two; someone Hall admired even if he wasn't a big success. Actually, Mr. Delaney was a drunk.

But hum the next verse in the background, Tom. It'll add a little mood to today's sermon, the main point of which is that God is not accountable to you, me or those big preachers for his taste in music.

Plenty of schools hand out degrees in church music, and that's a fine thing as far as it goes. Millions have been uplifted by finely tuned tones.

Unfortunately, neither a formal education nor a lifetime of practice in putting on airs and putting on arias can assure you of success in satisfying the most discriminating member of the audience: God.

Think of it like this. There are different levels of music appreciation.

A child thinks his pounding on a three-note Fisher-Price xylophone is beautiful ...

But that noise isn't appreciated by his father, who thinks that for real musicianship you can't beat Bruce Springsteen ...

But that noise isn't appreciated by his next-door neighbor, who has season tickets for the Huntsville Symphony ...

But that noise isn't appreciated by a connoisseur of the London Philharmonic ...

But that noise isn't appreciated by the conductor of the London Philharmonic, trying for perfection and falling just short in practice after practice.

Then there's God, to whom the vibrations emanating from all those instruments are beside the point. He's listening on a different level, hearing the vibrations not of reed, string and vocal chord, but of heart, soul and mind.

To God, reed, string and chord are just ways to express what's inside. Sometimes he likes what he hears; sometimes he doesn't. And he finds what he likes at all levels, from Fisher Price on up.

He finds what he likes being played on all sorts of instruments, from guitar, flute and harp to screwdriver, potter's wheel and a dry-erase marker in the hand of an inspired second-grade teacher. He finds good music where he will.

And human audiences cannot tell whether God's giving a thumbs up. They can't see what he sees, can't hear what he hears.

Knowing this is how things are, the best we performers can do is assume that those around us are making beautiful music, to which we may be tone deaf. Make that assumption even if you see a Clayton Delaney, picking out the lovesick blues.

Sing it, Tom:

"It made a big impression on me, although I was a barefoot kid

They said he got religion at the end and I'm glad that he did."

*"The words of a man's mouth are deep waters, but the fountain
of wisdom is a bubbling brook." Proverbs 18:4*

08.02.2003: There's at least one difference between a creek and a church

The creek is everything it ought to be. The spring water is clear and cold. Even with mercury and humidity at 90, it takes willpower to plunge in. The children happily splash within seconds of their arrival. The adults walk in gradually, torturing themselves anew over each sensitive bit of flesh.

I am on vacation this week, lounging at my in-laws' home in a small Southern town, and trips to the creek have been much requested.

The creek is easy to get to, off the main highway and up a dirt road. It has a sandy beach. It has beds of shells. It has a rope tied high in a cypress tree that swings out over a deep green pool. It has a current quick enough to float you downstream. It has bream and shellcrackers. It has shade. It has that calming gurgle.

Because it is accessible, and because it is a fine creek, this is a popular place. I was noticing this earlier in the week, up to my waist in water, while I swung the rope up to the next Tarzan candidate.

Some people arrive with a carload of kids and use the creek as a baby-sitter. Some arrive with a deck chair and sit in the shade, people-watching. Some arrive with a 12-pack and a major thirst. Some arrive with rod and bait. Some arrive with snorkels and fins. Some arrive with a McDonald's sack and don't leave the car at all but just look at the creek as they eat. Some cruise past in bass boats.

For the most part, these creek lovers seem to get along, but you have to know that a cannonball from the rope is annoying to the fisherman trying to work a nearby pool. Or that the rowdy teens aren't what the lady envisioned when she set her lawn chair near the shore. I'm sure these cross purposes bring some cross words, but for the most part people realize nobody has a lock on the creek. Everyone is welcome; please pick up your trash.

Your church is not so different from the creek. Amid the heat and humidity this world generates, it is a place people long to be. They all want the life-giving water around which the church is built, but they come with different visions of what church life is about. Sometimes cross words are exchanged between these very different churchgoers, but for the most part they realize that Christ invites all.

Here is one way, though, that the creek and the church are different. Those folks rubbing sunburned shoulders at the creek have only to get along, to tolerate each other for a few hours. They can grit their teeth or roll their eyes if need be. Those folks at the church are going to be together for a lot longer. Forever, even.

Tight-lipped tolerance is not enough. There must be love. There must be a celebration of differences.

Even if some boisterous newcomer does a hallelujah cannonball smack dab in the middle of my meditation.

"He saw heaven opened and something like a large sheet being let down to earth by its four corners. It contained all kinds of four-footed animals, as well as reptiles of the earth and birds of the air. Then a voice told him, 'Get up, Peter. Kill and eat.' 'Surely not, Lord!' Peter replied. 'I have never eaten anything impure or unclean.' The voice spoke to him a second time, 'Do not call anything impure that God has made clean.' "
Acts 10:11-13

11.12.2004: The test of a good pie isn't found in the trash can

When I was a kid, Mom made pies. Not every day, but she did her duty as part of a generation of mothers who believed in pies. Maybe this is what is wrong with America today – too many french fries and not enough pie.

Mom made chocolate, coconut, lemon, apple, cherry, peach, walnut, pumpkin É and at least one other flavor.

That other flavor is the topic of our sermon today.

My sisters had more talented palates than I, and this became apparent when the mellow smell of nutmeg and cinnamon wafted from the kitchen. If Mom placed on the table what appeared to be a pumpkin pie, I reached for the Cool Whip and was ready to eat.

My sisters, though, reached for the trash can. They wanted to be sure the pie really was pumpkin. See, Mom sometimes also baked sweet potato pie, which looked and tasted like a very close cousin of pumpkin. The sisters were convinced there was an important difference, and while they loved pumpkin, they refused to eat sweet potato pie.

Mom wasn't saying which flavor she'd made, so their solution was to check the trash can. If it contained an empty can of Libby's pumpkin, they were ready to eat. If not, they passed on dessert.

This made no sense to me. If you couldn't tell without the clue of an empty can, the best plan seemed to be just to dig in. I mean, it wasn't the label that excited my taste buds - it was the pie itself.

I'm sure if they'd tasted it, they'd have seen it was good.

I didn't tell my sisters this, because their reluctance sometimes meant more pie for me.

But enough about dessert; I'm making myself hungry.

John, the apostle whose writings are so simple and so deep, composed a long passage about testing the spirits to see whether they are from God. This testing involves looking for love, because "everyone who loves has been born of God and knows God."

But how do you recognize that love? John says, "If anyone has material possessions and sees his brother in need but has no pity on him, how can the love of God be in him? Dear children, let us not love with words or tongue but with actions and in truth."

Sorry to change the subject again, but I keep thinking about that pie.

Look at it like this: You'll be put in contact with a lot of people this week. Some will be sent to you from God, others won't. Each person is a slice of pie, and your job is to figure out which slices are tasty.

Too often, our solution is to use labels alone – Baptist, Catholic, Adventist – as the measure of which pies are good. If that's your sole criterion for spiritual relationship, you'll miss out on some of the delicious spirits God is sending your way.

If you're in tune with God, just take a bite and judge every pie on its own merits – does it taste like it came from God's kitchen?

I am willing to tell you this because, if you pass up some of the loving souls God sends your way, it doesn't mean more pie for me. No matter how you slice it.

SECTION NINE:
THE ELEVEN-MONTH CALENDAR

"From whose womb comes the ice? Who gives birth to the frost from the heavens when the waters become hard as stone, when the surface of the deep is frozen?" Job 38:29-30

11.30.2002: God's breath can start an ice storm, but his love can warm your heart

The harvest is in. Isn't that what Thanksgiving signifies? The farm-based tradition lingers, in a way. This weekend, in non-agricultural homes across the nation, from Minnesota to Alabama, refrigerators are stuffed fuller with Tupperware and Corningware bowls than at any time of the year.

Yes, the harvest is definitely in, and winter cannot be long in arriving.

Minnesota is already having high temperatures in the teens, forcing some Minnesotans to wear long-sleeved shirts. Here in Alabama we've dipped below freezing and are worried about snow flurries shutting down our society.

If not for the strong symbolism that Christmas has spread across most of the season, winter would not seem much like a biblical time of year. There are, in fact, no explicitly wintertime Bible stories.

The apostle Peter warmed his hands at a fire while waiting to see if Jesus would be condemned, but that seems a minor point. Our mental images of the Crucifixion don't turn it into a winter ordeal.

The apostle Paul warmed his hands at a fire on the island of Malta. It was cold, but that was because it was raining and Paul was already drenched from being shipwrecked.

The patriarch Jacob complains of being cold, but only while telling his father-in-law about what a miserable career he's had as a herdsman.

In Chronicles, some guy named Benaiah "went down into a pit on a snowy day and killed a lion."

There are a few mentions in prophecies and a sprinkling of proverbs, and that's about it for cold in the Bible. Snow is used more to evoke an image of whiteness than of winter.

This is natural when you set a book in the warm climes of the Middle East. Nazareth, in North Israel, is 2 degrees closer to the equator than Huntsville, in North Alabama.

Combine that factor with a few fire-and-brimstone sermons, and the Bible just seems more of a warm-weather text.

As we head into the ice age, however, there is this passage to consider, from Job 37:

"God's voice thunders in marvelous ways; he does great things beyond our understanding. He says to the snow, 'Fall on the earth,' and to the rain shower, 'Be a mighty downpour.' So that all men he has made may know his work, he stops every man from his labor. The animals take cover; they remain in their dens.

"The tempest comes out from its chamber, the cold from the driving winds. The breath of God produces ice, and the broad waters become frozen. He loads the clouds with moisture; he scatters his lightning through them. At his direction they swirl around over the face of the whole earth to do whatever he commands them.

"He brings the clouds to punish men, or to water his earth and show his love."

As the breath of God causes the temperature to fall and the clouds to swirl during these next few months, may that final phrase be enough to warm your heart.

Even in Minnesota.

"When a king's face brightens, it means life; his favor is like a rain cloud in spring." Proverbs 16:15

03.08.2003: There's no telling which year it was, but surely God created in March

I have an open mind about whether the world is 6,000 years old or 6 gazillion. My favorite theory about this is that God created the world 15 minutes ago, with our memories – and the fossil record – already intact.

However, I feel fairly certain that Archbishop James Usshur made a mistake when he painstakingly calculated in the 17th century that the world began on Sunday, Oct. 23, 4004 B.C.

Not October. Surely God scheduled his creation for a week in March.

It is the perfect time for creating. Walk into the back yard during these final days of winter and you are in a world that is without form, and void, where darkness is upon the face of the muck and mud that somehow replaced last summer's flower beds.

The twisted, naked limbs of the trees might be leftovers from some prior creation – once vibrant but now frozen into gargoyles that are slowly losing pieces of themselves to every stiff breeze.

And yet, if you could stand motionless in this yard until the end of March, your eyes closed tight while around you swirled the magic of rain, wind, sun, honeybees and the Lord God Almighty, your eyes would open on a new creation.

The gnarled trees would be clothed in the green of Eden. Not because they somehow discovered that they were shamefully naked, but because their creator inspired such joy that they slipped into party clothes.

You'd see deathly dark beds of mud now reclaimed by a victorious army – resurrected rainbow warriors holding high the banner of their maker.

You'd feel a delicious warmth. You'd think at first that it came from the sun glowing in a blue sky, where pure clouds flew like cherubim, silently singing, "Gloria!" But then you'd realize that the warmth flowed from the pores of every bit of matter surrounding you, be it animal, vegetable or mineral.

When you opened your eyes and did a slow turn to take it all in, your heart would rise within you as if it wanted to fly out and join the cardinal flashing through the forsythia.

You would know then that it must have been March when God created. And if the meaning of March was not known before creation, then surely from that year on creation defined what March meant.

I do not know how you would respond to this epiphany. I do not know how long you would stand there after your eyes opened, whether you would laugh, cheer, sigh or pray.

I suspect, though, that when you first moved your feet it would not be to go back into the house. You'd stride toward the garden shed or the garage, looking for a shovel, Roto-tiller, trowel or lawnmower.

That warmth from God's creation would have seeped into your soul, and you would know that in some small way you wanted to be part of it, to shape it and enjoy it.

A few months later you might remember the Adamic promise that the cursed dirt would produce only thorns, thistles and sweat.

But not now. Not in March.

"Later, knowing that all was now completed, and so that the Scripture would be fulfilled, Jesus said, 'I am thirsty.' A jar of wine vinegar was there, so they soaked a sponge in it, put the sponge on a stalk of the hyssop plant, and lifted it to Jesus' lips. When he had received the drink, Jesus said, 'It is finished.' "
John 19:28-30

04.12.2003: That unique Easter odor of vinegar is in the air

Many of the Easters since I was a child have included a simple little kit. You can buy one at any grocery store, in the rainbow-colored display at the end of the "seasonal" aisle.

With our Paas egg-coloring kit and a dozen hard-boiled Jumbo Grade A's, we can turn the kitchen table into a wonderland of brilliant creations a day or two before the holiday.

Actually, the most we usually achieve is 10 eggs dyed in various pastel hues, plus one that cracked during the boiling process and a 12th that some artist-to-be tried to dye orange on one end and purple on the other. Our Easter eggs are never as brilliant as the ones on the Paas box, but they are still a favorite bit of the season. We eat about half of them, and invariably end up throwing the rest away. Still, it's cheap fun.

To use the Paas kit, which has been sold every Easter for more than a century, you dissolve each dye tablet in a cup of vinegar, then dip your egg in the color of your choice.

Because of this, vinegar is the smell I associate most with the coming of Easter. I'm sure there are other smells – a glazed ham, a waxy chocolate rabbit with one ear nibbled away – but they announce that Easter is here, not that it is still approaching. One whiff of vinegar with its unmistakable tang, and you know we're not quite ready for Easter morning in all of its glory.

That sour, cutting aroma of vinegar was probably the last thing Jesus smelled during the dark weekend before the first Easter morning arrived in all of its glory.

In fact, the vinegar was shoved in his face at his absolute darkest hour, when from the cross Jesus moaned, "My God, my God, why have you abandoned me?" It was the middle of the afternoon, about 3 p.m., but God reinforced the fact that it was mankind's darkest hour, too, by plunging the Earth into pitch darkness.

In the moments after his lament, someone in the crowd below the cross raised a sponge on a stick to Jesus' lips. It was soaked in sour wine or wine vinegar, perhaps to ease the dying man's pain or to slightly resuscitate him.

Jesus cried out one more time, and then he gave up his spirit with the aroma of vinegar still in the air.

Smell is a powerful time machine, able to transport you back to a particular moment where your nose first experienced a certain combination of molecules. Surely there is no vinegar in heaven, where nothing ever spoils, but if there were I wonder if a single sniff would remind Jesus of that awful weekend.

I don't suppose the good people at Paas ever pondered any of this. They just recommend vinegar because it makes an egg hold the dyes better. That doesn't mean that you can't think about it, though, and impart a little extra value of your own to the cheap little egg-dying kit. When the kids smell that rancid odor, just remind them that it's a signal – something spectacular is about to happen.

Even if your eggs look no more like the beauties on the Paas box than mine do.

"Josiah was eight yeas old when he became king, and he reigned in Jerusalem thirty-one years .... He did what was right in the eyes of the LORD and walked in all the ways of his father David, not turning aside to the right or to the left."
2 Kings 22:1-2

06.14.2003: Here's what Dad would really like for Father's Day

Tomorrow is Father's Day. So what does Dad want? Almost certainly not a necktie – but if you've already wrapped one up for him, don't worry. Dad knows it is the thought that counts.

Almost any gift will please a good father. If he thinks about it long enough, though, here are some of the gifts that would please him the most:

To see his children become independent. When a small child lets go of Dad's hand in a crowded store and runs off to a different aisle, that is not independence. Sure, Dad wants his children to know what path they'd like to travel and to strike out on it, but he also wants to know as he watches them disappear that they have the skills and the strength to walk that path until it takes them where they want to go.

To know that if he is out of sight of his children, they act exactly the same as when he can see them, as if the rules he has given them have taken root deep within.

To see his children become purposeful. A little boy with the goal of playing professional basketball is not purposeful, even if he has a spurt of talent and growth that take him to the NBA. A maturing boy who realizes that he was placed in the world for more important things than playing basketball, that's purposeful.

To see his children learn to clean up a mess. Not just to stuff toys under the bed, but to look at chaos and have the determination and fortitude to turn it into order. There's a bit of God-liness about that ability, whether it shows up in an overgrown back yard or a corporation's tangled flow chart.

To discover that his children have become spiritual. Not just religious, not just saying prayers because they've been taught to, or even saying prayers because they believe there's a God up there somewhere, but saying prayers because they believe that they have something to do with God and that it is in his plane that their lives have the most meaning.

To see his children put another person before themselves. Not because they know it wins brownie points with spectators, or because they are in a good mood, or even because that other person is lovable ... but because his children have realized that the center of the universe is not simply wherever they happen to be standing.

To know that his children understand him, at least a little. To understand that when he utters the age-old mantra, "This is going to hurt me more than it is you," he is serious. To understand that his discipline is inseparable from his love.

It is probably too late to give Dad all of these gifts this year. The necktie, the cordless drill or the barbecue-sauce-of-the-month membership will be fine for now. He will accept them with a smile.

Remember, though, that there are other gifts a good father sincerely hopes for. Give them to him, and you'll probably please your heavenly father at the same time.

"At least there is hope for a tree: If it is cut down, it will sprout again, and its new shoots will not fail. Its roots may grow old in the ground and its stump die in the soil, yet at the scent of water it will bud and put forth shoots like a plant. But man dies and is laid low; he breathes his last and is no more." Job 14:7-10

10.14.2000: Autumn's coming on, and soon your true colors will be revealed

You may think of yourself as a mighty oak, unshaken by the wind and unmoved by the passing years, but in reality you're more like a single leaf of a sweetgum tree.

And autumn's coming on.

Leaves are green because they're full of chlorophyll, a green pigment that's crucial in photosynthesis. But autumn's coming on, and each day there's less of the sunlight needed for photosynthesis. So the chlorophyll is breaking down, letting a leaf's true colors emerge.

They're brilliant, those yellows and reds and oranges, but they're also the colors of death. Without chlorophyll, the food supply is cut off, and soon a leaf changes from a bustling bit of nature to a bunch of dead cells, twisting in the wind, waiting for the inevitable.

It happens to people, too.

Without the Son's light they wither and dry up, and their true colors emerge. Sometimes that can seem like a beautiful life, full of freedom and self-sufficiency and a kaleidoscope of good times. But autumn's coming on.

Some crusaders think you can save these people by eliminating their fall colors. So we wage wars to stamp out drinking and drugs, we march to close abortion clinics, we legislate against "colorful" behavior.

Some good comes from the crusades, sure, but in the end it's about as effective as painting autumn leaves a pretty springtime green.

Some religious bean counters think you can save these people by keeping their names written on a church roll. So what if they rarely darken the church doors, never lift a hand in service and put more thought into their fantasy football team than into their religion? At least their names are in the book.

Some good comes from the association, sure, but in the end it's about as effective as stapling fallen leaves back on the branches.

Some people think that they can find their own path to enlightenment, so they let go of any organized religion and sort of glide through life. Some leaves, after they let go of the branch, glide along in twisting paths so lovely that it can look as if they know where they're going, but they end up on the ground as surely as if they'd plummeted straight down.

People can fall in as many ways as there are leaves on a sweet gum.

But here, luckily, the autumn metaphor falls apart. In the sweet gum tree, the dead leaves will be replaced by fresh spring foliage. That cycle is a wonderful spiritual metaphor in itself, but those new leaves can't save the fallen, decayed ones. Come spring, they're still dead. And if you're a sweet gum leaf in this metaphor, that's not very comforting.

Rejoice, then, that while sunlight won't revive faded leaves, the Son's light will revive faded souls. If you're living out on a limb and you can feel the color draining from your life, it's time to turn your face to the Son.

Autumn can be pretty, in a melancholy way, but in the Son's light every day is spring.

"This is the day the LORD has made; let us rejoice and be glad in it." Psalm 118:24

10.21.2000: Some will boo, but God's people can make better use of Halloween.

It's a howling shame that God's people don't celebrate Halloween better.

We're splintered on this holiday. One branch celebrates it shallowly, like I did as a child, with cheery American icons of pumpkin and ghost and witch, trick-or-treating and candy overdosing. It's a Hallmark Halloween.

Another branch looks into Halloween a little more deeply and, troubled by its roots in Celtic rites, steers clear of any observance. Some rustle up a "harvest party" instead, with faceless pumpkins and spookless costumes. Of course, those old Druids had harvest parties, too.

Another branch, smaller but determined, wages a direct counter-attack on Halloween. They reach out, especially to teen-agers, with bloody events and blunt names like "Hell House" or "Judgment House." You want scary, we'll show you scary! Think of it as "Sinners in the Hands of an Angry God Part 2."

There must be a better way to approach Oct. 31. Call me weird, call me haunted, call me possessed, but I think I see it.

I wish we could blend America's traditions on this day with those of Mexico's El Dia de Los Muertos, "The Day of the Dead." It would take a generation to catch on, but it would be for the better.

Different regions of Mexico celebrate differently, and I suspect that some places turn it into more of a show for tourists than an honest expression of beliefs. Still, we can improve our own Halloween if we:

Make Oct. 31 a day to honor the dead. Some parts of Mexico have midnight parties in the cemetery to clean and decorate relatives' tombstones.

Make Oct. 31 a day to look our own death in the face. Being unafraid of death is supposed to be a central Christian sentiment, but in American society we tend to be so terrified of dying that we rarely even talk about it. I'm drawn to the Dia de Los Muertos custom of eating a sugar skull or skeleton decorated with my name, symbolically showing contempt for any power that death thinks it might have. Ditto for the devil.

Make Oct. 31 a day to declare that we have nothing to fear. Witches? Vampires? Goblins? Ghosts? God's people can take these icons of fear and darkness and reduce them to goofy costumes that even children can wear. It doesn't have to mean that we believe in these ghoulies; it can mean that we laugh at them, that we have conquered our fear of the dark because we are lit from within.

If we can pull it off, wouldn't that make a wonderful Halloween?

I know there are objections.

I know about the fears that teens will dip into the occult.

I know about the real Satan worshipers out there; I once was offered the job of ghostwriting the biography of a satanic high priestess turned Christian, and she told a gory story.

But I also know that God is bigger than our fears, and that even Oct. 31 is a day the Lord has made.

So, however you mark it, happy holiday to you and yours.

"When I was a child, I talked like a child, I thought like a child, I reasoned like a child. When I became a man, I put childish ways behind me." 1 Corinthians 13:11

10.26.2002: Just a few nights of Halloween, and then we'll grow into adults

We were born in light, but right now we crave darkness. It scares us, but the things we will do tonight would not have the same thrill in the sun's happy glow. We lift the curtain every few minutes to test the darkness.

Finally the purple-orange afterglow melts from the horizon. It is dark enough. We put on our masks. We do not want to show our true faces. Tonight we will be sinister and powerful, something all others had better fear and flee.

Out in the dark, we quickly form into groups with other mask-wearers. Partly we are afraid of being alone, but partly we know that only a gang can keep our actions from seeming shallow, silly and pointless. Isolated, we would not last as long before retreating to the light.

Our costumes slow us down. We sweat and stumble, but if someone talks of shedding his mask, the rest of us mock him.

We try every house that appeals to us, every house whose dark porch and silent interior doesn't scare us off. At even the darkest, scariest houses, at least one of our band tries to goad the rest into knocking. Sometimes this works. We don't want our gang to mock us.

When a front door swings open under our rapping, we hang back, none of us wanting to be the center of attention if this adventure goes sour. We shoulder our friends forward, though, until someone ventures the first "trick or treat." The rest of us echo it behind our masks.

Sometimes the doorkeeper is costumed as we are. Sometimes he recognizes us despite the masks and calls us by name, and we are embarrassed that he knows we are not what we seem. This makes us tighten our grip on our masks, fearing exposure.

We get exactly what we want from these houses. Treats, sweets, treasures to hoard and trade and gorge ourselves with. More treasures than we can possibly consume. In their wrappers they are bright as jewels, and we think them just as valuable. We know from past nights of prowling that soon we will be sick of these treats, but that just leads us on in our quest, knocking on new doors in hopes of untasted varieties. Maybe the next will be tastier, longer-lasting, more satisfying.

Besides, we are children, and Halloween only comes once a year. Soon enough we will be adults, and then we will not wear costumes to disguise our inner identities.

We will not be edgy when someone sees beyond our masks. We will not seek out groups for security. We will not let the members of our groups goad us into things we know better than to do. We will not knock about in strange, dark places for the treasures we imagine are behind their doors. We will not hoard beyond our ability to consume. We will not sicken ourselves yet keep asking for more of the same – new experiences, new highs, new treats. We will put away these childish things in just a few years, when we are too old to trick-or-treat.

Won't we?

"Hear, O Israel: The LORD our God, the LORD is one. Love the LORD your God with all your heart and with all your soul and with all your strength." Deuteronomy 6:4-5

11.17.2001: It's OK to crave trimmings more than turkey, but God is different

I like Thanksgiving dinner; you like Thanksgiving dinner. But I gotta admit, the turkey is really just sort of a centerpiece to give the table a proper holiday look.

Sorry, Tom. It's nothing personal.

I know the turkey is the main dish, and I eat a piece or two, but it's the trimmings I salivate for. Even the best bits of the juiciest Butterball are bland compared with the stuffing inside it and the stuff that surrounds it on the crowded table.

I'm pretty sure this isn't just my own holiday heresy.

Ask somebody else for a description of the perfect Thanksgiving feast and they'll gush about gravy and sweet potatoes and mashed potatoes and au gratin potatoes and vegetables and pickles and breads and cranberries and pies, and for each dish they'll be able to give you at least an outline of the recipe and a brief history of the relative who perfected it and why it's superior to the kind they serve in restaurants.

Turkey will be in there somewhere, but even if it is mentioned first, it won't get much gushing. People just don't talk turkey much.

Is that the way we are with religion?

Why do I attend church services, and how do I decide which services to attend? Ask somebody else for a description of the perfect church, and they'll gush about music and atmosphere and oratory skills and location and education programs and benevolence programs and gymnasiums and pew cushions, and for each point they'll be able to give you a reason it's superior to the kind they have at the church down the street.

God will be in there somewhere, but I doubt he'll be mentioned first. In fact, a lot of times it seems like God is just set out there on the table to complete our vision of the proper churchy tableau. God is not really what we like about our religion, but it just wouldn't seem right to leave him out altogether.

It's OK to treat a turkey that way. There's no law that says you have to eat the thing anyway, although if one of your loved ones cooked it, you'd be wise to at least have a nibble. Then if you want to fill up on cornbread dressing, fried corn and candied yams, go for it.

But God is not an entree. He is not even the main dish. God is our only source of spiritual nourishment. "In him we live and we survive," to quote a hymn.

Those other churchy things, the things people more often mention when the topic of religion is broached, are delicious or rotten based only on whether they bring us closer to God, so that seeing him and worshipping him we can be filled and he can be glorified.

I know that before the feast next week you will pause to pray, trying to concentrate as the smell of nutmeg and sage tickle your nose.

In that prayer, give thanks most of all for God. Pray that he will feed you daily, not just weekly, and pray that he will improve your palate so that if someone asks about religion you will gush about him, not just the trimmings.

"He humbled you, causing you to hunger and then feeding you with manna, which neither you nor your fathers had known, to teach you that man does not live on bread alone but on every word that comes from the mouth of the LORD."
Deuteronomy 8:3

11.26.2004: We can't make Thanksgiving leftovers last forever

Thanksgiving has been around for several hundred years, but it achieved greatness as an American holiday thanks to two key victories during World War II.

First, in 1941, Congress approved Thanksgiving as a legal national holiday. Second and more importantly, in 1945, Percy Spencer of the Raytheon Company invented the microwave oven.

This gadget transformed Thanksgiving from a single great feast into round after round of delicious and convenient leftovers. If the microwave oven was not invented specifically for Thanksgiving, it should have been.

I almost enjoy the second day's meal – plucked from a wall of Tupperware and aluminum foil that makes the refrigerator door hard to close – even more than the first. You fill a plate with dressing, turkey, casseroles and vegetables, pop it in the microwave and in two minutes it's Thanksgiving all over again. Gravy is a problem, but nothing's perfect.

Yes, Thanksgiving is one of the few times each year that I really enjoy eating leftovers.

In my spiritual life, though, I am not so picky. I am in the habit of getting by for days on end with leftovers, relying on them for my nourishment instead of seeking out new food.

Those verses I read from the Bible on Sunday morning ... I act as if they are still filling me on Friday. No need to eat anything new.

That mountaintop experience I had as a teenager ... I assume it is still nourishing my soul in middle age. No need to open myself to a new experience that might waft into my soul like the smell of fresh-baked bread.

That prayer I murmured last night just before I slept ... It was the spiritual equivalent of a quick midnight snack, but I treat it as if it were a three-course meal that can satiate me for the next 24 hours.

That devotional book I read four or five years ago ... As long as I remember its main points, why read another?

That communion with other Christians that lifted me two weeks ago — or was it three? ... I'm dragging now, so why am I not rushing back for another boost from those good brothers and sisters?

There's nothing inherently wrong with eating leftovers. The Puritans who helped create Thanksgiving would tell you it's a sin to waste food, and we should squeeze all the nourishment we can from our every spiritual experience. Eventually, though, even after a wonderful feast like we had this week, the leftovers will run out and we'll need to restock the kitchen and whip up something fresh.

David's sheep in Psalm 23 needed the shepherd to lead them to green pasture every day.

Christ's model prayer asks God for "daily bread," not weekly.

The wandering Israelites found that if you kept manna overnight it turned rancid.

One of the Beatitudes, distilling Jesus' philosophy of life, says, "Blessed are those who hunger and thirst for righteousness, for they will be filled."

That picture is not one of a man content to live on leftovers heated and reheated in a microwave oven, until there's nothing left but the hardened mashed potatoes scraped from the bottom of the bowl. No, it is a hunger that with God's help can turn every day of your life into a new spiritual feast, each one more deeply delicious than the last.

So keep cooking.

"Teach us to number our days aright, that we may gain a heart of wisdom." Psalm 90:12

12.28.2002: Dropping the ball all year has left me unprepared for a countdown

Everyone is anxious, ready for the big countdown before the ball drops in Times Square. But wait – I'm not ready! Not after the way I've dropped the ball all year.

Can't we postpone the countdown?

Ten. I still haven't come to grips applying the Ten Commandments in my public and private life. Yes, they're a rock-solid moral foundation, but Jesus said they weren't enough. When I read Christ's words about how looking at someone with hatred in my heart is tantamount to murder, I'm left to wonder whether Judge Roy Moore needs a bigger rock.

Nine. I have been no more grateful in 2002 than most of the 10 lepers Jesus met one day. I am certainly not that one in 10 who stops, seeks out his healer and says thank you for the gifts of health, happiness and a bright future. The Bible notes that the one thankful leper was also a Samaritan – a half-breed outcast. Does the fact that I am an American instead of a Samaritan make it harder for me to be humbly thankful? Do I act like I deserve whatever blessings come my way?

Eight. I'm still not doing much about the world's ark-to-water ratio. Tally up Noah and his wife, plus three sons and their wives; eight souls were all that survived the Genesis flood. This made for a low ark-to-water ratio. Today, I know that the number of believers is teeny within a world population of 6.25 billion according to the U.S. Bureau of the Census. Yet most days, I act as if that ratio is OK by me.

Seven. I haven't even worked up to forgiving people seven times, let alone the seven times 70 that Jesus called for.

Six. I haven't learned to contain my own hours of work and leisure within six days of the week, leaving God that one remaining day he asked for as "a day of sacred assembly." I am undeservedly smug about any week in which I give him more than an hour or two.

Five. I am so unlike that boy with the luncheon of five loaves and two fishes. Instead, I look at the meagerness of what I have, then at the size of the crowd and decide I need all five loaves to satisfy my own hunger. I never give God the chance to show that he could use them to feed 5,000.

Four. I am so unlike Zacchaeus, that tax-collecting cheat so convicted by Jesus' teaching that he promised to pay back four times anything he'd stolen from his customers. Dollar-for-dollar equality still concerns me more than do expressions of love and joy.

Three. I am way ahead of Simon Peter. He only denied his Lord three times with the sound of a rooster ringing in his ears, and regretted it almost immediately. I can't even count how many times my mouth ignorantly denies the same Lord.

Two. I still want to serve two masters – at least – even though Jesus told me I have to pick one.

One. I know my days are numbered, but I need at least one more year to get myself together. Lord, help me to count you as No. 1, every day.

SECTION TEN:
CHRISTMAS

"Simeon took him in his arms and praised God, saying:
'Sovereign Lord, as you have promised, you now dismiss your
servant in peace. For my eyes have seen your salvation,
which you have prepared in the sight of all people, a light
for revelation to the Gentiles and for glory to your
people Israel.' " Luke 2:28-32

12.01.2001: Remembering those who waited, we begin Advent in good company

These early days of Advent are about waiting. These nine
could tell you about waiting:

Zechariah: Eight months ago my wife had a baby. He came
straight from heaven. No, really! John is growing so fast – today
he let go of my leg and stood by himself. And smart – he looks at
me with those dark eyes as if he has something important to say.
I know I am too proud of my little John. But I am waiting too.
John's Aunt Mary tells my Elizabeth that she too is going to have
a baby – straight from heaven just like my John. I can hardly wait
to see what these two cousins will do for Jehovah. Together may
they reunite our people, O Lord.

Star seeker: East and West are far apart, this I know. Always
I have waited for heavenly signs that you in the West would not
credit even if I explained them. But last night my waiting ended.
We sorcerers saw a sign at which even the West will not long
laugh. Today I begin a journey to a bright star that I am told will
unite East and West, North and South.

Simeon: Many old men are waiting to die, but I wait happily.
The Spirit of God revealed to me that before my death these dim
eyes will see his Messiah. Oh, that my eyes may close with that
as their last image.

Anna: Do I know waiting? I was widowed in the seventh year
of my marriage, and now I am 84. That is a long time to wait. But
I have not given up. I practically live in the temple these days.
Think me silly, but I hate to leave it even for a moment. The Spirit
tells me that Messiah is coming. What if I miss him? Silly? I may

be 84, but sometimes I am as giddy as a maiden waiting for the bridegroom to come.

A crippled boy: For six years, maybe seven, I have waited for a cure. Everyone in the city looks down on me as they walk by. Each day is longer than the one before, but at night the dream comes. It is so real: A kind man comes to me. He asks if I wish to be well. In the dream I always answer yes, and he commands, "Rise!" Then I wake up to another long day. Oh, to hear that voice in daylight, and know it is not just a dream.

God: Since Adam's lips touched the fruit, I have waited for this. Soon the Earth will know true life once more.

Satan: Since my belly touched the dust, I have waited for this. Soon God will know death for the first time.

Joseph of Arimathea: I don't want you to get the wrong idea. I'm not morbid. I know I am young. I know I have much to live for. But, yes, I felt a calling to buy that tomb in the garden over by Jerusalem. My friends tease me and say I'm trying to join the Almighty early. I can't explain why, but the tomb just seemed ... right. I suppose if I wait long enough I'll find out why.

Mary: I am counting down the days, Jesus. It won't be much longer, my little king. I know I am not royalty, but I promise you that no queen will love you more. But what am I saying? The whole world will love you, won't it? Oh, I can hardly wait.

"When Herod realized that he had been outwitted by the Magi, he was furious, and he gave orders to kill all the boys in Bethlehem." Matthew 2:16

12.06.2003: At his birth and death, the Herods hated Jesus

Jesus knew he was hated. Toward the end he talked about it to his inner circle, quoting the Psalms: "Those who hate me without reason outnumber the hairs of my head; many are my enemies without cause, those who seek to destroy me." He wasn't moping. The hatred didn't alter his plans. He had felt the hatred from the beginning.

The first official response to his birth was Herod the Great's decree to execute every baby boy in the Bethlehem area.

Why such hatred?

Herod was King of the Jews, as decreed by the Roman senate and confirmed later by Octavian, who beat out Marc Antony as heir to Julius Caesar. Even though Herod confessed he'd backed Antony, his good friend, Octavian saw that Herod was the man for the difficult job in Palestine.

What Octavian couldn't see was the mental instability of Herod, a man who divorced and banished his first wife to clear the way for his second – only to later murder her and much of her family. If seers from the East said a baby in Bethlehem was to be a mighty king, the jealous Herod would have no pangs about stopping the upstart with extreme force.

One scholar estimates 20 babes fell under Herod's edict. Did any survive besides Jesus? Most did not, for in Matthew's account we hear an awful sound: "Rachel weeping for her children and refusing to be comforted."

The tiny Jesus was delivered from the hatred and the tears echoing behind him, delivered and taken to Egypt, where centuries before another baby had survived a king's decree of death. Survived to become his people's deliverer.

Soon an angel brought word that the King of the Jews was dead. He'd been through 10 wives, fathered 14 children, killed his firstborn, botched a suicide try, suffered through arteriosclerosis and oozed into the depths of every political intrigue in the region for decades. He had rebuilt in new splendor the Jerusalem temple, even though he was not by birth a Jew, but an Edomite, or descendent of hairy Esau.

When Joseph returned to Palestine, most of Herod's territory was ruled by a feared son, Archelaus. To avoid Archelaus, the holy family went north to Galilee, where a lesser son, Antipas, ruled. Rome did not let Archelaus stay long as King of the Jews, but Antipas endured. It was Antipas who beheaded Jesus' cousin, John the Baptist.

And it was Antipas, in Jerusalem for the holidays a couple of years later, who stood face to face with the survivor of the Bethlehem slaughter. He tried to coax a miracle from Jesus, but when the man had nothing to say to him, he roughed him up, dressed him in a robe befitting a "King of the Jews" and laughingly sent him off to die. His father would have been proud.

But why such hatred?

In the Herods you see jealousy, ambition, madness, lust, violence, vanity, boredom, pain, impulsiveness, narcissism and delusion.

The Christ came to end all that. No wonder the Herods hated him. But it's not just the Herods, is it?

"When Jesus landed and saw a large crowd, he had compassion on them, because they were like sheep without a shepherd. So he began teaching them many things." Mark 6:34

11.25.2000: With such a big crowd at the mall, Jesus never made it to the Hallmark

Jesus went to the mall the other day. I warned him it was the busiest weekend of the year, but you know Jesus – always wants to go where the people are.

He was just going to look at Hallmark for some cards, the ones that promise you a future gift of some chore or service. You know, "Happy holidays. This card entitles you to a free car wash." Something simple and practical, he said.

But he walked into the mall through the Dillard's entrance and got bogged down by this woman who said he was exactly the size of her husband and would he mind if she eyeballed a couple of sweaters against him. He was a good sport and pretty soon she'd told him her name was Doris and introduced him to her sister-in-law and her sister-in-law's mom and a couple of neighbor kids they'd agreed to watch because the parents were both on second shift. They were about to take the kids to get a cookie as a bribe for a bit more whineless walking, so they insisted Jesus come along, their treat.

That's when they got separated, because this bunch of teen-agers was hanging out by the cookie place, and one asked where Jesus got his sandals, and he started talking to them about clothing and they were telling him how they each had their own look and he said, "I know, but people have to get past the clothes to really see that," and they thought that was cool for an old guy.

But pretty soon the teen-age magnetic pull kicked in and the group got so big that the guy in the cookie store asked them to please move on. This one girl followed Jesus for a way. He didn't say what that was all about but she started crying and he gave her a hug and she went to the restroom to fix her eyeliner.

So Jesus started toward the Hallmark but he noticed a sale at Waldenbooks on religious books and wondered what that meant so he walked toward the back and saw Doris' neighbor kids in the children's section and they asked if he'd read to them and other kids sort of crept in until it looked like story hour at the library.

But then a lady asked him for help finding a cookbook and Jesus said he didn't work there and in about 10 seconds word spread and the parents all came scrambling for their children and you could hear the lectures on the importance of not wandering off.

Jesus made one last try for the Hallmark, but he took a wrong turn and ended up in the food court and decided he was hungry since he'd never gotten that cookie. The gentleman in front of him in line came up 42 cents short and was trying to decide what he and his wife could share but Jesus laid two quarters on the counter and before you know it he was sitting at the table with that couple and people kept stopping to listen and Jesus had to raise his voice to be heard and the crowd got bigger and a customer complained because he couldn't find a place to sit and someone called security and they asked Jesus to leave and everybody went back to eating and shopping and walking around in circles.

The mall people were nice about it. They told Jesus he just needed to schedule a time if he wanted to do a program.

But now's not a good time, they said.

Not at Christmas.

"But the angel said to them, 'Do not be afraid. I bring you good news of great joy that will be for all the people. Today in the town of David a Savior has been born to you; he is Christ the Lord.' " Luke 2:10-11

12.07.2002: On a mall visit so short, Jesus never did find out about 'the gift of love'

The other day Jesus decided to give the mall one more chance. I reminded him what happened last time he went amid the December frenzy, but you know Jesus – thinks everyone deserves a second chance.

He spent the first five minutes stuck at the counter of a jewelry store, trying to get a sales associate to explain a banner about "Giving the gift of love." He tried to loosen her up with some joke about how he'd have to revise his parable of "The Pearl of Great Price" since it looked like there were a lot more than just one, but then a more promising customer walked in so he strolled on down the corridor.

He saw another banner, pointing to the central atrium for a pageant called "The True Meaning of Christmas."

By the time he got there the show was just starting. A few folding chairs were left in the back row by the fake trees, so he slipped in quietly on the end. Most of the audience appeared to be parents of the half-pint pageant cast.

Apparently the kids were from some church up the road, and you could tell some were acting under protest. Video cameras were rolling, though, so the show must go on.

A little blonde with a Reynolds Wrap halo was telling two boys in bath robes, "Do not be afraid. I bring you good news of great joy that will be for all the peoples."

There was an awkward silence as the boys just stared at her, then Jesus said out loud, "Amen! Joy has come."

He was shushed by a lady two rows up in a red "Joy to the World" sweater. Then the little angel took control, herding the shepherd boys off stage. "You have to go to Bethlehem and see Jesus," she told them.

Then pretty much the whole cast gathered around a plywood manger. A teeny preschooler in a sheep costume saw all the red camcorder lights and bolted down the aisle.

Jesus was the first to react. With one arm he scooped up the passing boy and swooped him into his lap. "And whose lost lamb are you?" he asked. While sheep boy was deciding whether to cry, the woman who had shushed Jesus said, "Mine, thank you very much," and snatched him away with one of those grim faces that aggrieved mothers do so well.

She carried the boy back to the stage and had a word with the pageant director, who had a whisper with a security guard, who circled round and tapped Jesus on the shoulder. The guard said, "I'm sorry, sir. We've had a complaint ..."

They walked out together, Jesus explaining something about being a great shepherd. I'd warned him it would end this way, with Jesus out on the mall sidewalk, talking to security while the Muzak played overhead.

Best I could tell through the scratchy speaker, that old Ricky Nelson song was playing. You know the one: "When I got to the garden party, they all knew my name, but no one recognized me, I didn't look the same."

You'd think they'd play something more appropriate for Christmas.

"The time came for the baby to be born, and she gave birth to her firstborn, a son. She wrapped him in cloths and placed him in a manger, because there was no room for them in the inn."

Luke 2:6-7

12.08.2001: Different planning could have made life go smoothly for God's son

This idea of sending divinity to Earth was a fiasco from the start.

You'd think an eternal, omniscient, omnipotent God would plan things better:

Jesus is born to a woman a whole lot less than nine months after she's married, so that for the rest of his life his enemies can sneer at the legitimacy of his birth. Why couldn't his parents have been some poor but honest couple with more stability and decency?

Jesus is born in a dive. Actually, since the inns of the day were mostly dives, Jesus is born in some grungy cave out back of a dive. Why couldn't God look ahead and delay the birth until after the census, or give Mary and Joseph some personal reason to travel to Bethlehem, so that they wouldn't be crowded out?

Jesus is born with a megalomaniac in charge of the government, so that soon Mary and Joseph have to run for their life. Why couldn't God let Herod choke on a fig or something so that Jesus could grow up in Israel instead of Egypt?

These seem like such simple matters to have taken care of. Why did it all have to be so harum-scarum?

Let's say you're going to put your kid on an airplane for a trip by himself across country to Grandma's house. You plan for everything that might go wrong. You want Dexter to get there safely, so you make lists and give him instructions and calculate the best routes and make sure the attendants understand that he's going to need some attention. You might even find out what Grandma will wear when she meets him at the airport.

If you and I can plan things that well for our children, why couldn't God lay out a smoother path for his?

And it wasn't just Jesus' birth that was a logistical mess. Read any of the

Gospels and note how ineffective his adult ministry was. Some people believe what he says, but a lot more walk away in a huff, including most of the opinion leaders of the day who could have helped him spread the word.

Jesus' lasts three years in the limelight, then is destroyed.

Look at all of the obstacles and problems and aggravations he faced, and you might think, what a waste of potential.

You might wonder, too, about something else.

Let's say you're a believer in God. You're leaning on him, praying to him, urging him to handle your life and give you guidance and direction.

This is the same God who let Jesus go through life without a steady job or dependable friends or a roof over his head.

Are you sure you want to put your life in the hands of a God whose plans aren't any slicker than that?

Well, OK. It's your life. But don't say I didn't warn you. And don't complain if your life isn't as smooth as you'd like it to be.

God may plan for you just like he did for Jesus.

I guess things eventually worked out OK in Jesus' case, but there's no telling what you'll be dragged through if you let God lead.

"Jesus did many other things as well. If every one of them were written down, I suppose that even the whole world would not have room for the books that would be written." John 21:25

12.13.2003: Revisiting the 12 days of Christmas for real guys

You've heard plenty of sermons on how Christmas is all about God making a visit to the real world, arriving with no special privileges.

OK, you say, I get that. I'm a real-world kind of guy. But as a real-world kind of guy, what you really want to know is, what's that visit by Jesus ever done for me?

How about a dozen quick examples?

On the 12th day of Christmas, my true Lord gave to me …

Twelve crops of fruit. There's a new one every month coming out of the tree of life that grows in heaven É or maybe all 12 grow year-round. Either way, it's a lot better than that membership in the Fruit of the Month Club your cousin gave you last Christmas.

Eleven real-world guys who were willing to die because they believed Jesus was more than just a storyteller who was good with his hands. They were fishermen, accountants, ruffians, a doctor – at least one of them was the kind of guy you'd have gotten on with real well. Think about that when you read the messages they left behind.

Ten thousand guardians. That's a description used of how church life is supposed to be. Actual numbers may vary, but the idea doesn't – Christians take care of each other. Help it happen, guys.

Nine beatitudes, those pithy, one-sentence sermons that offer a better way to look at life than an eye for an eye. No, their purpose is not to get me stepped on out there in the real world, but it does take some major muscle to follow them.

Eight months wages worth of bread, produced from thin air by Jesus to feed a hungry crowd. You like to think you're a good breadwinner? Try that trick. Can't do it? Then respect the unreal power he showed while walking around in the real world.

Seven times 70 as the minimum number of times I can drop the ball and still expect other Christians to forgive me. That means the pressure is off, leaving only a grateful desire to do the best I can.

Six days out of seven to go about my real-world chores each week. That's a pretty generous split when you're dealing with the creator of the world.

Five golden words. Actually, they don't even have to be golden, just intelligible. The Apostle Paul says speaking five intelligible words in church is better than speaking thousands of words in some fancier language. For real-world guys who don't talk much, that's a comforting principle.

Four easy-to-read biographies about his life and death. Matthew, Mark, Luke and John definitely aren't chick books, even if John does talk a lot about love.

Three days of death for him that turned into an eternity of life for me. And you. And maybe every real-world kind of guy we bother to talk to about him.

Two simple choices. Believe he was God's son like he said. Decide he wasn't and go about your real-world business whatever way you choose.

And a savior hanging in a bare tree.

"You are all sons of God through faith in Christ Jesus."
Galatians 3:26

12.22.2001: Do you think I should bother sending a card to cousin Amy?

Should I send Cousin Amy a Christmas card, or would some secretary just flip it into the trash, unopened? That's what would happen if I were in her place.

Her place is a pretty nice one. Amy's maiden name is Grant. It's one of the biggest names in Christian music, with enough Grammy and Dove awards to fill a museum. That museum would need another wing, of course, because last year she married Vince Gill, one of the biggest names in country music, with just as many awards. The only question would be whether to call it the Grant-Gill museum or the Gill-Grant museum.

In marrying Vince, she became my Cousin Amy.

No, really.

Vince Gill was born in Oklahoma in '57. His father was Stanley Gill, whose mother was Virgie Beaver Gill, whose father was Newt Beaver, whose parents were Isaac and Mary Beaver.

Isaac and Mary begat 11 children besides Newt, including William Henry Beaver, who begat Minnie Bell Beaver, who married William Henry Bigham and begat Mary Jo Bigham, who married James Mendenhall and begat three girls and a boy named Doug. That's how I got begat.

One of my sisters collected all of that history, and it means Vince Gill and I are fourth or fifth cousins. I think.

Now, Vince has the most beautiful voice in Nashville and plays a mean electric guitar, but I've been a fan of Amy Grant's for a couple of decades, since before she had any of those awards. I treasured her debut album in college, before CDs were invented, and could still sing you most of its songs in my unique style.

So I'm tickled to claim her as my fifth cousin by marriage.

That's a pretty tenuous tie. It takes more than a genealogical chart to make you family. For one thing, both parties have to want a relationship, and I'm afraid that even if I sent her a Christmas card, Amy Grant wouldn't have the time for that. Be real: She just finished a big Christmas tour, she and her husband have a baby to coo over ... a fifth cousin by marriage doesn't rate much investment of time or emotion. Shoot, I don't even keep up with my first cousins.

But let me remind you that the situation is a lot different between you and God. Especially if the last time you acknowledged him was last Christmas, and you wonder whether it's worth the effort again this year to approach someone you barely know.

As you wonder about that, don't make the mistake of acting like God is just your fifth cousin by marriage. You need to know that the Almighty is ready and waiting to carry on a relationship with you, and that from the start he will treat you like a beloved child.

That's the gospel.

When you think about its implications, it's a bigger shock than if I sent that card to Cousin Amy and she called to invite me to Christmas dinner, saying, "Vince and I were hoping you'd write."

Unlikely. But that's how important even long-lost family members are to God.

"For we are to God the aroma of Christ among those who are being saved and those who are perishing. To the one we are the smell of death; to the other, the fragrance of life." 2 Corinthians 2:15-16

12.10.2004: Who'd buy potpourri that smells like Christmas?

In the hard-sniffing world of Acme Potpourri Inc., every nose knows this is D-Day. Fortunes can be made and lost, reputations polished or tarnished by the decision about a recipe for the new Christmas potpourri. A formula that will soon fill thousands of fragrant, ribboned bags. A formula worth millions of dollars to Acme.

The executive committee will hear three proposals, then pick the one that best captures the essence of the season.

Team One's proposal is "Sugarplum Vision." It begins with a base of cocoa and vanilla, over which are sprinkled bits of apple, peppermint, wintergreen, orange, cinnamon and clove.

"Not bad," the chairman says, "but we're making potpourri here, not candy. Every time little Johnny nibbles on the product, we'll lose a customer. Mothers won't stand for that. Next."

Team Two has taken a different approach with its "Christmas Mountain" – pine cones and oak leaves, mosses and acorns, three shades of red berries, a touch of eucalyptus, a smattering of redwood duff.

"Aah," the chairman says. "Not novel, but nicely blended. Should work well with the male clientele. Perhaps we could market in that direction. Worth considering. Next."

Team Three's proposal, "Heavenly Holidays," smells like a 50/50 mixture of the Team One and Team Two creations, but with a sprinkling of something else.

"Ginger?" the chairman guesses, and as usual he is correct. "We tried that last year – let's move on."

And that's it. The Acme directors are ready for the most important vote of the business year.

"Excuse me, sir," a voice rasps from a back corner. "Have time for one more?"

It is Matthew, the ancient and semi-retired janitor. He's an odd sort, but gentle and harmless. "For you, Matthew? Of course," the chairman says, "But we need to keep it brief. What do you have for us?

The old man lifts a battered tin canister toward the chairman's face and unscrews its lid. The chairman's eyes narrow as his nostrils widen. "Why, it's beautiful, Matthew. It is absolutely the smell of Christmas. But what's in it?"

Matthew smiles an odd smile and passes over a yellowed sheet of paper.

The chairman reads aloud, his voice puzzled: "Barnyard dirt. Hay. Unwashed sheep. Unwashed shepherds. Donkey. The sweat of fear. Blood. Three kinds of imported tree sap. Soiled linen … Matthew, is this some kind of joke?"

Matthew shakes his head and replaces the lid on his canister.

"C'mon, what's really in this stuff, Matthew?" the chairman asks. "It's the most amazing thing I've ever smelled."

Matthew insists the canister contains exactly what is on his list. The chairman says that's impossible.

"Not impossible," Matthew says, "Difficult, but not impossible."

"What's the secret?" the chairman asks."Well," Matthew says, "when you mix it up it smells pretty awful. You have to let it settle for a long time before the true essence emerges."

"How long?"

"Um, 33 years," Matthew says.

"Matthew, there's no way we can wait 33 years to produce a scent," the chairman says, "even one this lovely. We've got to think about what's commercially prudent."

"I know," Matthew says softly, and then he pauses. "Shame, though, isn't it? All those people settling for a cheap imitation of the real thing?"

And then Matthew returns to his chair in the corner, and the executive committee turns to the business of deciding what Christmas will smell like this year.

"Jacob the father of Joseph, the husband of Mary, of whom was born Jesus, who is called Christ." Matthew 1:16

"He was the son, so it was thought, of Joseph, the son of Heli."
Luke 3:23

12.17.2004: Did Grandpa Jacob finally get to see the baby?

To say Grandpa Jacob wasn't exactly full of the Christmas spirit was an understatement. He wasn't in the mood to celebrate anything – not even with a new baby in the family. Especially not with a new baby in the family!

In fact, if you'd congratulated him on his grandson, he'd probably have glared at you until you went away. Not that people were lined up to offer congratulations. Business had been slow as news got around town about the circumstances surrounding that new baby.

Old Jacob's son had been a good boy, respectful, devout, proper. He'd learned the family craft well, and Jacob was proud to have such a son ready to inherit the carpentry shop. His Joseph was a bright star on the horizon, a promise of a wonderful future.

But then Joseph's young fiancee got pregnant, and Joseph ran off with her, and that star blinked out for Jacob. Joseph had told Jacob they were just making a short trip to register for the census, and Jacob had nodded his head, but the angry, heartbroken father had known even as he watched his son heading south out of Nazareth that he would not be back.

And for more than a year now, Jacob had been right. No sign of his disgraced son. No sign of Miriam, the girl who shared Joseph's disgrace.

They'll never come back, Jacob told himself again. He was a proud and stubborn man, but perhaps it was time to get past this catastrophe. Perhaps he should stop mourning his son.

Perhaps he should even pay a visit to his former friend, Heli, the father of Miriam. They'd talked and laughed together often after the agreement for a marriage was arranged. But that seemed an eternity ago, and Jacob and Heli had not spoken since the couple left town. Maybe Heli would lash out at him. Could he risk such a scene?

And then Jacob looked south and saw them, slowly walking into Nazareth. His Jacob looked a little older, a little harder, a little thinner. But Miriam – surely this could not be the same girl? She was fully a woman now, young, but no little girl. Then Jacob's eyes locked on the third figure, a curly-haired little boy balanced on Miriam's hip.

For a moment, Jacob wasn't sure what he should do. Turn his back? Go into the house and order his wife not to open the door? Then he felt his feet begin to move, pulling him toward the little family ...

Yes, this is a fanciful story, for the Bible says almost nothing about the grandfathers of Jesus. We know their names, Jacob and Heli. We know Jesus was mocked later as illegitimate. But the stories of the grandparents are lost in the brightness of this new star on the world's horizon.

I like to wonder though, about Grandpa Jacob and Grandpa Heli, and their unnamed wives, of course. I hope they all lived to see the baby and love him.

And I like to think that the baby, when he became a great teacher whose stories amazed the crowds, reached back into his childhood. And maybe he thought of his grandfather and his father when he told a story about a son who left home under horrible conditions, and about a father who ran to welcome him back when at last he came home.